THE ILIAD
AND ODYSSEY
OF HOMER

THE ILIAD
AND ODYSSEY
OF HOMER

radio plays by

KENNETH CAVANDER

BRITISH BROADCASTING CORPORATION

The Iliad was broadcast in the Living Language series of School
Radio in 1968, and the Odyssey in 1966 and again in 1969
Thursdays 2.0 p.m. Radio 4, 2 October–13 November.
Editor: Joan Griffiths

In order that this book should stand in its own right, and
not just as a record of a broadcast, sound effects are hardly
indicated, and passages from the original scripts that had to
be cut out, because time was short, have been restored.

The illustrations for the Iliad are by Swietlan Kraczyna,
and those for the Odyssey are by Charles Keeping.

© Kenneth Cavander 1969

First published 1969

Published by the British Broadcasting Corporation
35 Marylebone High Street, London W1M, 4AA
Printed in Great Britain by Cox & Wyman Ltd,
London, Reading and Fakenham

SBN 0 563 08535 5

Contents

Introduction

These radio dramatisations were prepared from the Greek of
Homer's *Iliad* and *Odyssey* for broadcasting in the Living Language
series of BBC School Radio. The Narrator's text follows Homer
very closely. Wherever possible the dialogue scenes have been put
together from lines, fragments of lines, and hints in the original
Greek. Only one episode, Part Five of the *Iliad*, is not taken
directly from Homer: the story of the capture of Troy was
reconstructed from references in the *Odyssey,* passages in the fifth-
century dramatists, and other traditional sources.

The long narrative poems now called the works of Homer were
first edited and written down some time after 700 B.C. and before
500 B.C. Nothing is known for certain about their author –
whether it was one man or many, or whether such a person as
'Homer' existed at all. The stories themselves are very ancient, and
were recited by professional storytellers who learnt them by heart
and went from place to place entertaining the communities of the
Greek world with these legends about their ancestral heroes.

The medium of radio is therefore an appropriate way to
reintroduce these tales to a twentieth-century audience. Composed
for the listener, not the reader, these stories of adventure and
heroism, high and low comedy, love and death, created (like radio)
moving pictures for the mind's eye. It was left to a later and more
literal age to replace the spoken with the written word. And so in
following Living Language with a book, the BBC is retracing the
same path first taken by these myths on their journey to a wider
audience.

Kenneth Cavander

ILIAD

I The Wrath of Achilles

CAST:

Narrator
Athene, goddess of wisdom
Poseidon, god of the sea
Zeus, father of the gods
Thetis, a sea nymph, mother of Achilles

Greeks
Agamemnon, their leader
Odysseus
Kalchas, a very old priest
Achilles
Helen

Trojans
Priam, king of Troy

NARRATOR: On the shores of the land of Troy, far to the east
Of Greece, a thousand ships were beached, pyramids
Of spears and swords, chariots and shields, lay
Scattered along the sand.
Here the armies of Greece had set up their camp.
For ten years they had fought and died on the plains
Of Troy, determined to bring home Helen.

Helen, the most lovely of all the women in Greece,
Had left her husband Menelaus, and sailed to Troy,
Where the king's son, Paris, kept her for his own.
Menelaus had called on his brother, Agamemnon,
And all the princes of Greece, to help him win back
His wife. And so they had shipped to Troy
The greatest army the world had ever seen,
And for ten years they had tried to take the city.

But they had failed. And now, in the tenth year
Of the war, the Greeks were dying of more than wounds.
A plague had struck the army, and many lay sick,
Unable to fight; the funeral pyres burnt by night
And day, and only one man could tell where the plague
Had come from, and what would make it end.
That man was Kalchas, the wise witch-doctor of Greece,
Who was so old his words came like the whisper
Of leaves in autumn. Odysseus went to see him . . .

KALCHAS: You ask what caused this plague.
The plague was sent by the god Apollo. It will not leave
The army in peace until the god is satisfied.

ODYSSEUS: What must we do?

KALCHAS: Agamemnon has a prisoner of war – a girl. Her father
Tried to ransom her, and Agamemnon refused.
So her father prayed to Apollo to help him,
And Apollo answered his prayer by sending this plague.

ODYSSEUS: But Kalchas, how do we . . .?

KALCHAS: Patience, Odysseus! Give back the girl,
And the plague will go away.

ODYSSEUS: And the girl's name?

KALCHAS: She is called Chryseis.

ODYSSEUS: Chryseis . . .

> *The assembly, murmurs, with Agamemnon's voice rising
> above them*

AGAMEMNON: I will *not* give up Chryseis! I fought long
And hard for my war prizes. I refuse to be robbed
Of something I paid for in blood!
> *Chorus of protest*

ODYSSEUS: Most noble Agamemnon, general and leader
   Of all Greeks. For ten years we have laid siege
   To Troy, and some of *our* blood has been spent
   As well. We are your friends, are we to fail now,
   And all die of sickness, just because of a *girl*?
AGAMEMNON: A girl brought us here – Helen!
ASSEMBLY: *Reaction* . . . Not worth it . . . Let her stay here . . .
   Go home . . .
ODYSSEUS: Achilles wants to speak. Silence! Let Achilles
   Speak . . .
   The reaction fades
ACHILLES: I know how Agamemnon feels. And I sympathise.
   I have treasure I won in this war, and I would hate
   To give it up. But this is a time when we must make
   Sacrifices . . .
AGAMEMNON: *I* must make them, you mean!
ACHILLES: We have made ours. We have fought for your brother.
   Chorus of assent
AGAMEMNON: Very well, very well . . . I will give up Chryseis.
   But I want a second princess in return – and I also
   Expect an ox-cartfull of gold, and ten tents
   Of pure silk . . .
ASSEMBLY: *Consternation* . . . Where is it to come from . . .
   All this . . .
ACHILLES: Most noble Agamemnon, I cannot decide
   Which is greater – your power over men,
   Or your greed for their possessions.
   Where are the Greeks to find all that treasure
   To give you? The spoils of war have already
   Been divided or sold.
AGAMEMNON: *Icily* Most excellent Achilles, if you want me
   To give up the princess Chryseis, I must have something
   In return. Now, I don't care who gives it to me –
   Whether it's you, or Odysseus here, or Ajax –
   But something I must have!
ACHILLES: *Even icier* My most esteemed lord Agamemnon, allow me
   To remind you, I am only here to help you and Menelaus –
   Yes, to help *you*, dogface!
   Gasp from the assembly
ACHILLES: Does that mean so little to you? Well, since you mean
   To keep for yourself all the war-spoil and glory,
   And let the rest of us have nothing – goodbye.
   I am tired of fighting, tired of piling up hoards
   Of treasure for you, and getting no thanks.
AGAMEMNON: Go on, then, Achilles, if that's how you feel.
   Run away. I won't go down on my knees and beg you

To stay. Since the god Apollo demands Chryseis
From me, my men shall go to your tent and take
Briseis, your own princess, and that will teach you
Who has the power here. It is I, Achilles,
I have the power – and you have nothing!
NARRATOR: As Agamemnon spoke, Achilles could feel
Two desires pulling opposite ways in his soul.
One told him to draw his razor-sharp sword,
Carve a path through the crowd, and kill Agamemnon;
The other held him back, and quenched his blazing
Anger . . . He was standing there, with his sword
Half drawn from its sheath when suddenly . . .
  Supernatural sound
Out of nowhere, standing behind him,
Was the goddess Athene. She tweaked his hair.
Achilles turned round in amazement, and saw her,
Saw the two burning eyes staring at him.
No one else knew she was there, but Achilles did,
And he trembled.
ATHENE: Obey me, Achilles . . . Keep your sword in its sheath,
And tame your fury. Do as I say and you will have
A reward, three times as rich as the one
Agamemnon takes from you.

NARRATOR: Achilles put away his sword, and without another word
He went back to his tent. There he told his friend
And fighting companion, Patroklos, to take Briseis
From the women's quarters and hand her over
To Agamemnon. Briseis wept as she went,
And Achilles could not bear to see her go. He ran
Down to a deserted stretch of beach, where he stared
At the grey and foaming sea, looking out
Over the endless waves . . .

ACHILLES: My mother, Thetis, spirit of the salt
Wave spray, listen to me. You know – you must know,
Because you are a goddess, what they've done to me!
Help me. I am born to live for only a short while
On this earth. In the few years that are given to me
I must win a lifetime of honour and glory.
But the Greeks hold me in contempt. I am nothing
To them. Nothing! Do you hear me, dear mother . . .?
THETIS: *As through water, an undersea sound* I hear you,
My son, from the ocean depths I hear you . . . And Zeus,
Supreme god on Olympos, shall hear from *me*!
NARRATOR: Thetis rose in a cloud of foam from the ocean,
And leaving a trail of rainbows across the sky

She flew to the top of Olympos where Zeus sat
On his throne. She knelt at his feet and begged him
For a favour. She begged him to avenge her son
Achilles, and send bad luck to the Greeks,
To make them wish they had never insulted him.
Zeus lowered his head as he listened, then he raised it,
Brought his great black eyebrows together in a frown,
And nodded once. His long hair swayed, Olympos
Trembled to its roots, and Thetis knew
He had granted her wish.
> *A peal of thunder*

That night, to fulfil his promise to Thetis,
Zeus sent a dream to Agamemnon, and when dawn came
Agamemnon sprang from his bed and quickly called
A council of war. All the generals were there –
Odysseus, Menelaus, Ajax, old Nestor,
And many others – but the place where Achilles
Should have been standing was empty.
> *Murmur of council*

AGAMEMNON: Listen, let me tell you my dream!
> *Council murmur quietens*

AGAMEMNON: It was a man, a very old and bearded man,
It looked a little like Nestor here . . .
> *Laughter*

AGAMEMNON: And this old man told me that today was the day
We shall capture Troy.
> *Amazed reaction*

AGAMEMNON: So today – I proclaim battle!
> *Cheers*

ODYSSEUS: But what about Achilles? Can we fight without Achilles?

AGAMEMNON: Can we fight? . . . We can, Odysseus, and we can *win*!
Let him sit in his tent like a sulky baby,
While we men win the war. Leave him there with Patroklos,
And perhaps, if we feel generous, we may bring them
Some toys from the city of Troy when we capture it!
> *Laughter*

NARRATOR: So the Greeks marched out, pouring from their camp
At the edge of the sea, and set out once more
To attack the towering walls of Troy. Their hearts
Sang with joy of battle. On that day they would rather
Fight and die than return to the land they were born in.
They came, like a fire that sweeps across mountains
When the forests are dry as tinder . . . they came,
Like endless flocks of birds – swans and geese –
That crowd the sky in autumn with their beating wings. . .
They came, like swarming clouds of flies that buzz

Over summer fields – numberless, a mass of moving bodies,
Tossing horse-hair plumes, flashing armour,
Spears and shields . . .

And on the walls of Troy, watching the Greeks advance,
Stood the cause of all the fighting, the wife
Of Menelaus – Helen.
And beside her stood Priam, King of Troy and father
Of his people.

PRIAM: So once again the Greeks are going to try to take you
Away from us, Helen . . . My old eyes can't see
From here. Tell me who's leading them today . . .

HELEN: Do you see that tall one, a huge bull of a man?
That's Agamemnon, a great king and a fearsome warrior.
He governs more men than any other Greek. And look,
Beside him, his brother Menelaus . . . who was once
My husband . . . Now, over there, do you see
Someone smaller by a whole head than Agamemnon,
But broad in the shoulder and chest – that's Odysseus,
A great leader of men. He knows how to make people
Do anything he wants, he's clever . . .

PRIAM: Who is the one, a real giant, towering over the rest,
A monster like a walking wall?

HELEN: That is Ajax, the toughest Greek of them all.
No one man can fight him alone.

PRIAM: But with one of the gods on his side a Trojan
Could defeat even Ajax . . .

HELEN: Oh Priam, I wish I had never left my home, I wish
I had never followed your son here. There would be
No war then, Trojans and Greeks would be living
In peace.

PRIAM: I did not want this war. But now too many have died
On each side. It will only end when one of us wins . . .

HELEN: Look, down there, your sons are going out . . .

NARRATOR: Beneath Helen and Priam the great west gates of Troy,
The Skaian Gates, opened wide, and the Trojan army,
Led by Hector and Paris, two sons of Priam,
Marched out. Hector's hair flamed like a tawny lion's,
Paris blazed like the sun . . .

Trumpets – men's chanting

HELEN: Paris – my dear love Paris! Be careful!
Paris . . .!

NARRATOR: But Paris could not hear Helen's voice
Above the din of chariots and men, the clash and clatter
Of armour, the pounding of horses' hooves . . .
At the sight of the Trojan army coming out to meet them

The Greeks stopped. Agamemnon told his men to wait
For his signal, and prepare themselves for battle.

Closer and closer came the Trojans like a wave
Of the sea, on foot, on horseback, running, riding,
And a deafening clamour rose in the air.
    Shout – trumpets
Agamemnon gave the signal, and they charged!
The two armies, glittering with bronze and steel,
Crashed together in the centre of the plain.
Shield battered shield with huge thuds, spears
Flew thick in the air, swords spat and sparked,
And helmets waved above the dust kicked up from the ground.
The yelling and shouting mingled into one great roar
Of killers and killed, dying and crying,
And the earth gushed blood.

While far beneath him the armies fought, Zeus
Picked up a pair of scales. In one of them he put
The fate of the Greeks, and in the other
The fate of the Trojans. Then he held the scales up
By the middle, and watched.
The scale that belonged to the Greeks sank down,
And Zeus thundered on high.

Below, on the ground, the Greeks trembled,
And a white flash of terror struck their hearts.
Neither Agamemnon nor Menelaus dared stand his ground,
Nor Odysseus, quick and crafty, nor mighty Ajax
With his shield like a tower, nor old Nestor,
Wisest of all the Greeks. The tireless work of Paris
And Hector, huge in his fury, drove them back,
Always back, towards the ships and the shore
Where their tents stood undefended.

Agamemnon, in desperation, prayed to Zeus ...
AGAMEMNON: Zeus, father of gods and men,
    Why have you done this to us? You sent me a dream,
    And I believed it! But now you swamp us in shame,
    And snatch away the victory you promised.
    Is it my fault? Have I been a miser with my sacrifices?
    Are a thousand oxen slaughtered on your altars
    Not enough for you?
    Save us, Zeus, if ever in the past I was generous
    In my gifts to you – do not let my Greeks
    Be massacred by the Trojans like this!
NARRATOR: Zeus heard and had pity on Agamemnon.
    He sent an eagle, of all birds the one most trusted

By men, with a young fawn in its talons.
The eagle swooped down and dropped the fawn
At the feet of Agamemnon, and at once the Greeks
Took heart. They saw that Zeus still cared for them,
And they turned and held back the Trojans.

For the rest of that day the battle raged, and when
Night came, it came as thrice welcome relief
To the Greeks – though the Trojans thought
They were winning, and were unwilling to stop.

The night brought the Greeks no rest, however.
They worked in the darkness, piling earth
In high ramparts to protect themselves and their ships.
Beyond the earth wall they scooped out a ditch,
A deep broad ditch with spikes planted like a row
Of jagged teeth, and the gods on Olympos
Marvelled when they saw it.

POSEIDON: Zeus, my brother, look at those Greeks!
  They're building a wall round their ships.
  What shall we do? They're going to win,
  In spite of what I had planned for them.
ZEUS: Poseidon, I'm surprised at you. There you sit,
  Shaker of earth and sea, and you're worried
  About a wall of dirt built by a few mortal men.
  One touch of your finger and it will all
  Come tumbling down.

NARRATOR: Meanwhile the Trojan watchfires twinkled all over
  The plain, and the Greeks knew from the sound of men
  Moving between the tents that there was something
  Planned for the next day. Whatever it was,
  It meant danger for the whole Greek army, and when
  At last the ramparts were finished, and the soldiers
  Slept, even then fear did not leave them.

They knew that in the sky Zeus was still awake,
Planning the fates of men, and many a warrior
Shivered in his dreams as he felt the hand of death
Touch his shoulder lightly.

ILIAD

II Fire at the Greek Ships

CAST:

Narrator

Greeks
Agamemnon, their leader
Achilles
Odysseus
Diomedes
Nestor, a very old man
Ajax, a very strong man

Trojans
Hector, prince of Troy
Andromache, his wife
Dolon, a spy
Servant

NARRATOR: The Greeks were asleep in their camp on the beaches
Of Troy – only the sentries were awake, the sentries
And Odysseus! Odysseus could not sleep. The Trojan
Watchfires strung like stars across the plain
Reminded him that the next day there would be more
Fighting. He decided to go out and spy,
And he woke his friend, Diomedes, a warrior
More feared by the Trojans than any except Achilles
Himself.
They dressed themselves in their armour, and each
Took a sharp two-edged sword, and a small shield
For close fighting. It was the middle of the night.
The only sound was the waves on the beach,
And the wind whistling across the plains from Troy.
Before they set out, Odysseus and Diomedes
Offered up a prayer.

ODYSSEUS: *In a whisper* Goddess Athene, listen, it's Odysseus
Calling your name – grant me a safe return
To the ships tonight, and let us do some great
Deed that will make these Trojans take notice of us!

DIOMEDES: *In a whisper* Goddess Athene, can you hear me?
It's Diomedes, and many a time in the past
You took care of my father. Take care of me now!

NARRATOR: Odysseus and Diomedes, armed to kill, left
The war-camp and picked their way like two lions,
Cloaked in black night, through the carnage,
The corpses, the armour broken and bent,
The caked blood.
        Their footsteps. Night sounds

ODYSSEUS: Ssh!
        Their footsteps stop

DIOMEDES: What is it?

ODYSSEUS: I hear someone. Listen.
        Single footsteps approaching, cautious

ODYSSEUS: Hide! Quick! Behind this broken chariot.
        Scuffle as they hide

DIOMEDES: He's coming this way. Suppose it's Hector! We'll . . .

ODYSSEUS: Ssh!
        Footsteps very close, crunching of sand, nervous breathing

ODYSSEUS: Now!
        Two great shouts overlapping, clatter of swords, shriek of terror

DOLON: Don't kill me! Don't kill me!

ODYSSEUS: Keep your voice down, or you'll die
For talking too loud!

DOLON: *Quietly, stammering* Yes, sir, yes, master, yes,
My noble lord, I won't say a word, I won't

Speak, I won't say anything just so long as you spare . . .

ODYSSEUS: Shut up!

> *Pause*

DOLON: *Whimpers*

ODYSSEUS: Now Trojan, by the point of this bronze sword
You feel tickling your throat, tell me . . .

DOLON: *Interrupting* Anything, sir, anything, I'll tell you
Anything . . .

DIOMEDES: Wait till you're asked, then, dog!

DOLON: Yes, sir, yes, I'm sorry.

ODYSSEUS: Thank you, Diomedes. The Trojan's teeth
Chatter so hard we can't get a word in edgeways.
Now, what is your name, and what are you doing
In the camp of the Greeks? Taking the midnight air . . .?
Or spying?

DOLON: My name is Dolon, and I was sent by Hector
To find out what the Greeks are planning –
Whether you mean to stand and defend your ships,
Or whether you mean to set sail because you're tired
Of war and killing.

DIOMEDES: Listen, friend Trojan, Hector may have sent you,
But now you're working for us. So tell us,
What are Hector's plans . . .? Quick, or you'll have
No head left to talk with!

DOLON: Hector plans to attack at dawn. Before first light!
He's going to take the ships by surprise,
Burn them all, and leave you stranded here
To be slaughtered one by one.

NARRATOR: Dolon was right. Hector had left the Trojan camp
And gone back to the city of Troy, where he spent
The night preparing his surprise attack
On the Greek ships. As the darkness began to give way
To the coming sun, he dressed himself from head
To foot in shining bronze, and put a great helmet
On his head. Then he went to his house to look
For his wife Andromache, and say goodbye to her,
As he did every time he went out to battle.

> *Door opening*

HECTOR: Andromache . . .! Andromache!

SERVANT: Master . . .

HECTOR: Where is my wife? I looked in her room,
And it's empty. And my son, Astyanax –
He should be asleep, but his bed is empty too . . .

SERVANT: My lord Hector, your wife went up to the battlements
To watch you leave for today's battle.
She took your son with her . . .

HECTOR: Which battlement?

SERVANT: By the Skaian Gate . . .

NARRATOR: Hector ran from the house, across the courtyard,
Through the broad avenues of Troy echoing
Strangely in the cold light before dawn, till he came
To the Skaian Gate. Up he climbed,
Five steps at a time, and there, on the topmost
Tower, he found Andromache, standing gazing across
The plains towards the sea, and holding asleep
In her arms little Astyanax, wrapped warm against
The wind that blew in from the east.

HECTOR: Andromache, why are you not indoors?
It's cold . . .

ANDROMACHE: Hector . . .!

HECTOR: You're crying!

ANDROMACHE: Don't you care, don't you have pity on me?
And if you don't pity me, at least think
Of your little son . . .

HECTOR: I do. I fight to keep you both safe.

ANDROMACHE: Every day that you fight – I die. I die,
Hector! I imagine the Greeks leaping on you,
Stabbing you, killing you!

HECTOR: I can fight any Greek in their army.

ANDROMACHE: Achilles?

HECTOR: What?

ANDROMACHE: Can you fight Achilles?

HECTOR: *Slightly evasive* Achilles sits in his tent these days,
And no one has seen him near the battle line.
I hear he is angry. Maybe he'll join our side!

ANDROMACHE: But suppose they trap you . . .

HECTOR: No, Andromache, no. It's I who will trap them.
Before the sun is up, my men will be there
At the trench, carrying fire. We'll burn
The Greek ships . . .

ANDROMACHE: Will you be there . . . when they burn the ships?

HECTOR: Of course. I lead the attack.

ANDROMACHE: I'm afraid, Hector, so afraid . . .
Baby cries, just awaking

HECTOR: Look, Astyanax is awake . . . Astyanax, say goodbye
To your father. He's going out to fight the Greeks.
The baby cries loudly. Hector and Andromache laugh

ANDROMACHE: It's your helmet, Hector, all that shiny metal
And huge horse-hair plumes waving in the air
Above him. He's frightened. Take it off.
Let him see your face.
Hector removes his helmet

HECTOR: There, Astyanax, now you see who it is . . .
     Crying stops
HECTOR: Smile for me now . . . Come here, I'll show you
  The Greek ships . . . That's where I'm going today.
  And look, behind you – Troy. Some day you'll grow up
  And you'll be king of all this, you'll be a great
  Warrior and a great ruler – much better than your father.
  You'll go out to war, kill all our enemies, and come
  Back with their armour. You'll make your mother
  Proud of you . . .
ANDROMACHE: Hector! No!
NARRATOR: Andromache took her son, and hugged him
  To her breast, smiling through tears. Hector
  Saw those tears, and touched her with his hand,
  Turning Andromache to face him.
HECTOR: Don't be angry with me, my darling. There is no man
  Born who can escape death. Go home now,
  And look after our house, and leave fighting to men.
NARRATOR: Without another word she obeyed. Hector
  Picked up his helmet and ran to join his troops
  In the plain below.

The Trojan armies were ready, and as the first light
Showed the way, they stole across the plain
To the ditch and the rampart built by the Greeks
The night before. As they came near the ships
Hector let out a spine-chilling yell, and his soldiers
Broke into a run. They hurled volley after volley
Of spears, and behind them came men armed
With burning torches, ready to throw them
Aboard the Greek ships and burn the tents.

But instead of the sleeping camp they expected,
They found the Greeks awake, prepared by the news
Odysseus and Diomedes had learnt from the spy.
And so, as Hector charged, shouting, at the head
Of his Trojan warriors, a line of Greek archers
Rose above the rampart with arrows ready
In their bowstrings.
Their captain of archery gave the command,
They drew their bowstrings taut, aimed, let fly
Their arrows – and those arrows made a cloud that dimmed
The sun as they went hissing towards the Trojan army.
The greatest archer in the Greek army was Teukros,
And Teukros now took aim straight at the heart
Of Hector. He aimed with all the care and skill
He knew, and he would have struck Hector dead

That instant, had not the god Apollo, ever watchful
Of the Trojans, turned the arrow aside. The point
Went deep into the chest of Archeptolemos,
Hector's brave charioteer, who was catapulted
Backwards out of the chariot. Grief and anger
Surged through Hector and he gave the reins
To the nearest man to hold and told him to watch
The horses. Hector himself leapt to the ground,
Glittering from head to foot in his armour,
Snatched up a huge rock in one hand, and advanced
Straight on Teukros. Teukros plucked
A barbed arrow from his quiver, and fitted it
On to his bow, but Hector hurled his rock,
And just as Teukros raised his bow to let loose
The arrow, the jagged stone crashed into his shoulder,
Just at the place where the collar bone joins
The ribs and a man can be hurt. The stone cut
The muscle, his arm hung limp down to his wrist,
And he crouched, unable to move, letting his bow
Slither to the ground.

Now Hector was like a ravening hunting dog
That snaps and snarls at the heels of a wild boar
Or a lion – running, circling, darting forward
And back – so Hector harried the Greeks on the ramparts,
Killing, killing everybody who stood in his way.
The Greeks fled. They were in panic, and the Trojans
Followed them up on the earth-wall, while Hector
Called for fire, fire to burn the ships and cut off
The Greeks' retreat from Troy.

Agamemnon ran from end to end of the battle line
Shouting above the din:
AGAMEMNON: For shame, Greek soldiers, for shame! Stand and fight!
Be men! In the name of honour – fight!
Don't let the Trojans beat us back!
NARRATOR: They heard his voice, and stopped in their tracks.
Then Odysseus stood like a rock and held his men.
Diomedes turned and lifted his flashing sword high.
Menelaus rallied his warriors, and King Agamemnon himself
Threw his fiercest troops into the oncoming ranks of Trojans;
The battle was joined again at the very edge
Of the Greek encampment, not a hundred yards
From the ships.
The mass of fighting men looked like a field of corn
Swaying and tossing beneath the gusts of a strong wind
While a cloud of dust and sand rose in the air

And dimmed the sun. Inch by inch, leaving blood
In every footprint, the Greeks forced
The Trojans back, and the fire that menaced their ships
Burnt out in the hands of the torch-bearers.
All day long they fought. Time and time again
The Trojans, with Hector at their head, made a fierce
Charge to break through the Greek lines, and always
The Greeks, led by Agamemnon, would throw them back,
Fighting desperately for their lives.

When evening came, both sides broke off. The Trojans
Went back to their camp in the middle of the plain,
And Agamemnon held a war council. The faces
Of his generals were worn and scarred with battle,
Sad with the loss of good men wounded or dead.
>   *Council murmur*
AGAMEMNON: Friends, I have lost too many men, and failed
Too wretchedly. I think, now, we shall never capture
The city of Troy. Let us take what we can
Of our war-spoil, save the rest of our men,
And sail home.
>   *Pause. Murmur*
NESTOR: My lord Agamemnon . . .
AGAMEMNON: Yes, King Nestor . . .?
NESTOR: I am the oldest here. I shall speak first.
I propose we try one last stratagem. I propose
We go to Achilles, and ask him to return to the fight.
ODYSSEUS: Why should he, Nestor?
NESTOR: To save his fellow Greeks.
ODYSSEUS: Then we have to offer him something, some lure,
Some bait.
AGAMEMNON: What do you suggest, Odysseus?
ODYSSEUS: General Agamemnon, I'm sure you can think
Of a suitably tempting gift . . .
NARRATOR: Everyone knew what Odysseus meant, and they agreed
To follow Nestor's advice. An embassy was chosen,
And they elected Ajax and the wily Odysseus to go
And talk to Achilles.

His tent was far away from the battle lines,
Because he wanted to keep his men apart from the rest
Of the Greek army. As they reached the tents
Where Achilles' men were encamped, Ajax and Odysseus
Could hear something strange. From one of the tents,
The largest, came the sound of a lyre, and laughter,
And song . . .
ODYSSEUS: Well, Ajax, it sounds as if Achilles enjoys

Himself while we go out to the war . . .

AJAX: How can he enjoy himself? There's nothing so good
As fighting, and fighting's not what he's doing.

ODYSSEUS: You would say that, Ajax, because you can't sing
A note yourself.

AJAX: I can make any man's head sing, Odysseus, with one
Tap of my finger.

ODYSSEUS: Well, be polite to Achilles. Tell him you like
His singing . . .

Louder

Achilles . . .! My lord Achilles . . .!

The singing stops

ACHILLES: Who is that? Odysseus!

AJAX: And Ajax . . .

ACHILLES: My dear friends . . . Come into my tent . . .

AJAX: I liked that stupid song you were singing, Achilles.

ODYSSEUS: That's enough, Ajax . . . ! Don't listen to him
Achilles . . . He lacks grace . . .
Good evening, Patroklos . . .

ACHILLES: Patroklos, bring us wine, put another branch
On the fire, and spread out more rugs . . .

NARRATOR: Achilles made his old friends welcome,
And they told him about the defeats the Greeks
Had suffered. Then Odysseus craftily turned
The conversation round to Agamemnon . . .

ODYSSEUS: And so Agamemnon offers, and hopes you will accept
His offer, to return Briseis to you. And Achilles –
He will do more, you know. He will give you ten
Treasure chests full of gold, twenty copper
Cauldrons, and twelve thoroughbreds that will win
Any race you care to name. And if we all get home
Safely, he promises he will give you one of his daughters
To marry. They are beautiful girls, Achilles,
I have seen them . . . Well, what do you say?

ACHILLES: Odysseus, you are a clever man, and when you speak
Your words seem to drip with honey. But I
Am a simple soldier. I have to say what I think,
And so my plain and simple answer to you is this:
Neither Agamemnon, nor any other Greek,
Will persuade me to fight the Trojans again.
There is no honour to be won at Troy. The brave man
And the coward get the same reward. I have spent
Many sleepless nights and much of my blood –
And look at me. I might as well be a slave!
Agamemnon has cheated me, dishonoured me, and I say
His gifts are poison to me! I would not marry

His daughter if she were the most lovely woman
In creation. I have always had two choices
In my life – either to stay and fight the Trojans,
Die here, and win eternal glory for my name – or
Go home, live a long life, and never be heard of
Again. I now choose the second, and I advise you all
To do the same. Sail home. You will never take Troy.

AJAX: But Achilles, I don't understand . . .

ACHILLES: What, Ajax? What don't you understand?

AJAX: A man will accept money to make up for a son
Or brother killed. But nothing satisfies you.
What do you want? Hasn't Agamemnon offered enough?

ACHILLES: Ajax, nothing Agamemnon offers could be enough.
Every time I think of him, the anger rises in me
And I choke!
I tell you, I shall never fight for the Greeks.
I shall only fight if I have to save my own ships
From burning.

NARRATOR: Ajax wanted to argue with Achilles, but Odysseus
Silenced him with a look, because he saw
There was no hope of changing Achilles' mind
That night. Sadly they returned to the war council
And told them of their failure. When they had finished
Diomedes leapt to his feet . . .

DIOMEDES: Agamemnon, why do we try to bribe Achilles like this?
Look, now he is more proud and arrogant than ever!
I say we can win without him! I say we should scorn
His help. Tonight we eat and drink and sleep.
Tomorrow we go out and fight the Trojans again,
And this time – we win!

Swelling applause

ILIAD

III The Armour of Achilles

CAST:
Narrator
Iris, the rainbow goddess

Greeks
Achilles
Patroklos, his friend
Menelaus, Helen's husband
Ajax, a very strong man
Nestor, a very old man

Trojans
Priam, king of Troy
Hector, prince of Troy
Paris, his younger brother
Asios, his uncle

NARRATOR: Dawn rose from her bed to begin the work of the day,
    Bringing light to the world of men and gods,
    And Agamemnon passed the order along to all the Greeks
    To arm themselves. He took his weapons – his great
    Shield, with its ten circles of bronze, his two spears
    Tipped with copper, and his sword. Then the Greeks
    Marshalled their lines at the edge of the camp,
    Charioteers keeping their horses in perfect trim,
    While the men on foot filed out in their dazzling armour.
    Then they all gave a shout, the heavens rang,
    And they charged.
    The Trojans were ready to meet them. Hector
    Was everywhere – now leading a fierce attack,
    Now rallying the men behind, and he flashed in the battle
    Like a bolt of lightning sent by Zeus.

    But no-one could stop Agamemnon. He drove the Trojans
    Back – back towards their city, and they fled
    In terror, while he picked off the stragglers
    Left behind in the rout.

    At the gates of Troy stood Paris, watching his army
    Ebb back like a tide to the safety of the great walls.
    He turned to Priam, who stood beside him, and spoke
    To the old king.
PARIS: Father, look at all this slaughter and bloodshed,
    Look at the waste of men and animals, all
    Troy's wealth squandered on this war. How can we
    End it?
PRIAM: My son, if you really want to end the fighting,
    I'll tell you how. Give back Helen.
PARIS: Give . . .! Give away the most beautiful woman
    In the world . . .?
PRIAM: Yes. You brought her here, you made her desire you,
    And for her sake all Greece is at war with us.
    If you really love your country, your brothers,
    Your old father, let Helen go back to Greece.
PARIS: Impossible! I love her. I shall never let her go!
    But I will offer as much gold and silver
    As Menelaus and Agamemnon can carry away
    In their long warships.
PRIAM: They'll never accept it.
PARIS: Then that will be their loss and their sorrow.

NARRATOR: Paris summoned his charioteer and told him
    To find Menelaus in the throng of the fighting.
    They sped through the battle lines, holding

A flag of truce above their heads, to make sure
No Greek would turn and attack them as they drove
Across the dusty plain.
At last they found Menelaus, drilling his soldiers
For a charge, and Paris hailed him with a shout.
The fighting died down, and the soldiers stood
And listened ...

PARIS: Menelaus, lord of Sparta and former husband of Helen,
Your wife belongs to me now, I won her fairly,
And she loves only me. I will fight to keep her,
And never willingly let her go. But I *will*
Make amends to you for the loss of your wife,
And so I hereby promise, in the presence of both armies,
To give you the greatest ransom the world has ever
Seen. Accept my offer. Let there be no more dying,
No more wounding, let our peoples live at peace.

MENELAUS: Paris, son of Priam, how can you ask me to take
Gold and silver in place of my wife? Nothing
Can buy back beauty, once it is lost. Your offer
Is an insult, and I hereby hurl it back
In your handsome face!

AJAX: And I too, Paris, I, Ajax, who never tire
Of fighting, I tell you to go home and wait,
Quaking with terror, in your room in Troy,
Because you will soon all be dead, all you
Famous Trojan warriors!

MENELAUS: Wait, Ajax, I have a better plan ... Will you fight me,
Paris, alone, in single combat? ... Well? ...
Do you accept my challenge?

PARIS: I do ... gladly ... Clear a space in the middle
Of the army. Let us test the strength of our arms,
And the sureness of our aim.

NARRATOR: The two men armed themselves with spears,
A clearing was made in the ranks of soldiers,
And they strode into it, glaring fiercely
At each other. The Greeks and Trojans fell silent,
Awed by the savage hate they saw in the warriors' glances.
First, Paris hurled his spear, and its shadow
Flitted across the plain towards Menelaus. The point
Struck his shield full in the centre,
But the shield stood firm, and the sharp bronze
Was blunted. Then Menelaus sent his own spear
Crashing into the shield of Paris. It went right through
And sliced into the buckles and chains of the coat
Of mail he wore beneath. But Paris swerved aside
And the cruel metal only grazed his ribs. Menelaus,

Furious at missing, lunged at Paris,
Reached out for his helmet, grabbed the plume,
And spun him round. He dragged Paris along
In the dirt, and Paris began to strangle in the strap
Of his helmet. He twisted and struggled, gasping
For breath. Then all at once the strap broke,
The helmet came away in Menelaus' hand,
And Menelaus fell backwards with a shout in the dust.
Paris scrambled to his feet, and ran for the safety
Of his own army. Everyone laughed to see
The two princes rolling in the crumbled earth
Of the plain, but when the men saw the rage
And shame in the heroes' faces, they quickly
Hid their smiles.

Agamemnon signalled the end of the truce,
And once more hurled himself into the battle.
Step by step, like a raging demon, he forced
The Trojan army into retreat.
They were just reaching the steep walls of Troy
When one of the Trojans, Koön by name, slipped to one side,
Escaping Agamemnon's sharp eye, and came up
On his flank. Koön flung his spear, and the point
Sliced through Agamemnon's left arm, below the elbow.
Agamemnon shuddered, but did not stop his onward rush,
And for a while he continued to fight. But as the blood
Dried in the wound sharp pains began.
Then Hector saw his chance, and like a hunter
Urging on his dogs he roared at the Trojans to chase
The Greeks back to their ships. He was like
The spirit of war itself, a terror to men, a walking
Living storm. The Trojans wheeled, and followed
Hector, and the god Apollo joined them, sweeping
Along the tracks of the battle, bringing fear
And despair into the hearts of the Greeks.

Now the Greeks were in retreat, and the Trojans
Followed, lashing their horses on, calling to each other
With a burst of noise that chilled the Greeks to the bone.
Like a wave of the sea, when a gale goads it
To fury, the Trojans surged forward over the plain,
Driving the Greeks in fearful turmoil back to their ships.

Meanwhile, Patroklos had left the tent of Achilles,
And was walking through the ships to watch the battle.
He stood on the top of the rampart, and saw the Greeks
Scattering in panic, and heard their screams.

He let out a groan of sorrow, and turned to run back
To the tent of Achilles.

PATROKLOS: Achilles . . .! Achilles . . .!
Achilles, the Trojans
Are at the edge of the camp. The Greeks can scarcely
Hold them back!
ACHILLES: Does it matter, Patroklos?
PATROKLOS: I'm going to help them!
ACHILLES: Can't they defend their own ships?
PATROKLOS: The best are hurt or dead. Agamemnon took a spear
Through his arm. And Odysseus cannot walk. The wounded
Lie where they fall, no-one looks after them . . .
ACHILLES: But my ships are safe, Patroklos, and I made up
My mind I would not fight.
PATROKLOS: Achilles, give me your armour!
ACHILLES: My what?
PATROKLOS: Give me your helmet, your shield, your breast-plate . . .
ACHILLES: Wait, Patroklos, wait . . . Now, why?
PATROKLOS: I'll dress myself in your armour, I'll go to the fighting,
And the Trojans will think it's you. They'll never
Stand and face Achilles himself, they'll run.
Please, Achilles, for the sake of our friendship . . .

NARRATOR: Patroklos begged so hard, and Achilles was so
Unwilling to refuse anything his friend asked,
That soon Patroklos was arming himself in the weapons
Of Achilles . . .
ACHILLES: But remember, Patroklos, you will show yourself
At the head of my men, you will turn the Trojans back,
But you will not go up to the walls of Troy . . .
PATROKLOS: Now the breastplate . . . Thank you . . .
ACHILLES: Patroklos, did you hear me?
PATROKLOS: One more buckle, here . . . Yes, Achilles, of course
I heard you.
ACHILLES: What did I say?
PATROKLOS: Turn the Trojans back.
ACHILLES: But do not go up to the walls of Troy.
PATROKLOS: Yes, yes! Not up to the walls . . .

NARRATOR: Dressed from head to foot in the armour of Achilles,
Patroklos walked out of the tent, collected a band
Of soldiers, and set out for the edge of the camp,
Where the Greeks were trying to hold the Trojans back.
PATROKLOS: *Shouting* My friends, remember who you are.
Soldiers of Achilles! Men of war! HEROES!
Show these Trojans how soldiers of Achilles *fight*!

NARRATOR: These words fired their courage into a blaze,
 and they raced
To meet the mass of the Trojan army. A roar went up
From the watching Greeks, and the air shook with the din.

Patroklos himself led the way. His spear
Gleamed and darted in front of the fighters,
And the first man he struck fell dead in the sand
On his back. Wherever he went Patroklos brought
Stark terror, and soon he had driven the Trojans
Back from the ships, back from the Greek encampment.
The Trojans, screaming with fear, crammed the paths
To the city, their horses strained to run faster,
Faster, speeding for safety behind the great stone
Battlements.
Patroklos raged in pursuit, blowing a storm of fear
Through Trojan hearts as he drove them back. Now
The Greek ships were safe, and he should have remembered
The words of Achilles . . .

ACHILLES: *Memory voice* Do not go up to the walls of Troy . . .

NARRATOR: But the battle bore him along like froth on the crest
Of a wave. He chased the fleeing Trojans,
And forgot Achilles' warning. He thought only
Of winning glory, more glory, and never saw
The dark face of death staring straight at him.

At the gates of Troy stood Hector, keeping his horses
On a tight rein, not certain whether to drive
His chariot into the fight, or tell his men to turn
Back to safety. As he stood there, a man came
And spoke to him. He looked like Hector's uncle,
Asios, but he was really the god Apollo, disguised.

ASIOSAPOLLO: Hector, why are you holding back? Look, there is
Patroklos. Here is your chariot. Hunt him down!

NARRATOR: Hector did not answer. Without a word
He lashed his horses into a gallop, and plunged
Into the thick of the fighting to reach Patroklos.

Patroklos saw him coming, and stopped his chariot.
He jumped to the ground, gripping his sword
In his left hand. With his right, he picked up
A jagged rock, and waited for Hector. As Hector
Swooped down on him Patroklos hurled the stone,
And found the mark he aimed for – Hector's charioteer.
The rock's edge crashed into his forehead,
And shattered the bone. His eyes flew out and fell
In the dust at his feet. Like a diver, the charioteer

Plummeted backwards out of his chariot,
And his spirit flitted away to Hades. Patroklos
Rushed forward to take hold of the corpse and strip
The armour, but Hector pounced from the chariot
Like a lion and stood over the body.
While the battle raged around them like the east
And north wind battering a wood in a valley,
When pine trees and ash and oak sway and groan
In the storm, those two – Hector and Patroklos –
Faced each other.
There the god Apollo, ranging the battle lines,
Found them. With one blow of his fist he stunned
Patroklos, who shuddered. His eyes rolled, and Hector,
Seeing his chance, thrust his spear deep
Into Patroklos' stomach. He fell with a crash.
The bronze point went through his body and jutted out
At his back, and a howl of fright went up
From the Greek army as they saw him fall. Hector
Knelt down beside him . . .

HECTOR: No, Patroklos, you will never take the city of Troy,
Never take our women captive to Greece, or steal
Our freedom away. Instead, Patroklos, the vultures
Will eat you here . . .

PATROKLOS: *Dying* Good, Hector, good . . . You've won . . .
Apollo helped you, and you've won. But I tell you now,
Death stands near you – yes, your fate is fixed . . .
You can't escape . . . Achilles. Achilles will be . . .
Your fate . . .!

NARRATOR: As he spoke, death shrouded his eyes, his spirit
Left his body and flew down to Hades. Then Hector
Stripped away the armour and would have dragged off
The body, if Menelaus, fighting on the far edge
Of the battle, had not seen him, and brought
Ajax to his side to help him.

MENELAUS: Ajax! Quick! They've killed Patroklos.
Let us save his corpse . . .

AJAX: Who has his armour?

MENELAUS: Hector.

AJAX: Stop him!

MENELAUS: This way . . .!

NARRATOR: Hector was meaning to lop away Patroklos' head
And leave his body for the dogs to eat, but Ajax
Was bearing down, holding his huge shield like a tower,
And Hector backed off. Ajax came up and stood guard
Over the body, and Menelaus ranged himself beside him,

But even then Patroklos was not yet safe. Hector summoned
His brothers Paris and Aeneas, and full of fury
They charged Ajax and Menelaus, meaning to kill.

Meanwhile, old Nestor, who had seen everything,
Hurried back to the Greek ships to bring the news
To Achilles.

NESTOR: Achilles! . . . Where is Achilles?

ACHILLES: Here, Nestor . . . What happened?

NESTOR: Achilles – the Trojans . . . they . . .!

ACHILLES: What? Did they take the ships? Did they burn them?

NESTOR: No. Patroklos sent them running, but . . .

ACHILLES: What then?

NESTOR: Hector killed him!

ACHILLES: Killed Patroklos?

NESTOR: Yes.

ACHILLES: *Pause. Shout of pain*

NARRATOR: At Nestor's words Achilles crouched in agony,
Tearing the ground in grief, pouring red dust
Over his hair, disfiguring his handsome face.
He clutched his head, frantic with sorrow, and could not
Hold back the great sobs that tore at his body.

NESTOR: Achilles, they're fighting over Patroklos now.
Hector has taken the armour – you must hurry.
Save him for burial at least!

ACHILLES: How can I save him? Patroklos took my armour,
And now you say Hector has stolen it. *How*
Can I save him?

NARRATOR: The Greeks in the plain still tried to drive Hector
And Paris away from Patroklos' corpse. But those two
Stood like fierce lions guarding their kill,
And would not be driven away . . .

At his tent Achilles held his head in his hands,
Speechless, except for the groans, like no
Human sounds, that racked him. Then he heard a voice . . .

IRIS: Achilles, listen. It is Iris,
The rainbow goddess, servant of Hera. She pities you,
And begs you to save Patroklos' body.

ACHILLES: What can I do? I have no armour. I have no spirit
Left in me . . .!

IRIS: Walk on the rampart, and you will see the power
Of the gods at work!

ACHILLES: What will happen? What can I do unarmed?

NARRATOR: But Iris had vanished. Then Achilles sprang to his feet,
And strode along the beach to the ramparts,
Where he could see the fighting. As he went

The goddess enveloped his head in a cloud of gold,
And above the cloud leaped a tongue of flame,
Like the flame that spurts up from a city
When it is besieged by enemies and lights a signal
At night to let its neighbours know it needs help.
So the fire shot up from Achilles' head, as he stood
At the edge of the camp, in plain view
Of the whole army. There he raised himself
To his full height, and gave a shout. That shout
Was like the sound that blares from the brass throat
Of a trumpet. It rose in the air above the roar
Of the battle, and froze the hearts of the warriors.
Horses pricked up their ears, men stood transfixed.
They stared behind them, up at the rampart, and saw
In the distance – Achilles, his hair and head ablaze
With leaping tongues of fire. Once again he shouted,
The Trojans turned and ran, and the Greeks swiftly
Snatched up the body of Patroklos and rescued it
From the battle.

As Achilles watched his friend being carried along
Limp and dead on a stretcher, he made a promise
To himself.

ACHILLES: My father, Peleus, will never see me walk into
His house – I shall never rest or cease fighting –
Until I have killed Hector, and all Troy pays
With sorrow and tears for your death, Patroklos.
I swear it. I swear revenge!

ILIAD

IV Achilles Takes Revenge

CAST:
Narrator
River Scamander
Thetis, a sea nymph, mother of Achilles

Greeks
Agamemnon, their leader
Achilles
Achilles' horse

Trojans
Priam, king of Troy
Hector, prince of Troy

NARRATOR: Just as a lioness will mourn for her cubs
  When she returns to find that a wandering huntsman
  Has taken them – so Achilles raged and paced
  In his grief for his friend Patroklos, and swore
  Again and again to levy a toll in Trojan lives
  For his death.
  Alone, far from the battle, he crouched over the body,
  And there his mother, the goddess of the sea,
  Thetis, found him.
THETIS: Achilles, my child, listen to me.
  You must go out and fight, not waste your days
  In useless grief.
ACHILLES: How can I fight, mother? I have no armour.
  Hector took it!
THETIS: Look.
          Clatter of armour
ACHILLES: Where was this made? It glows like fire.
THETIS: This armour was forged in the workshops of Olympos.
  Hephaistos, the fire god, hammered it himself.
  Wear it. You will be the first, and last, to do so.
NARRATOR: The armour Thetis had brought glinted and gleamed
  On the ground with terrible unearthly light.
  It was beaten out of the purest bronze, and the fire
  That tempered it was the molten lava of earth itself.
  Greatest of all was the shield, on which Hephaistos
  Had worked a whole universe. He showed a sun and a moon,
  Comets and planets, and constellations of stars.
  There were cities of men, buildings and people,
  Soldiers marching out to war, farmers ploughing,
  Weddings and harvests, wild beasts and farm animals,
  A palace for a king, a feast with guests and food,
  And a sacrifice for the gods.

  Achilles snatched up the armour, and then
  Like a hawk that swoops down from snowy Olympos
  He strode through the camp in search of Agamemnon.
  He found the general, with his wounded arm cradled
  In a sling, seated in conference with the princes
  Of Greece.
ACHILLES: Friends, I come to bid you to a feast.
  A feast of fighting . . . Agamemnon, let us lay aside
  Our quarrel. What good has it done us?
AGAMEMNON: Achilles, I gladly accept your invitation. We all do.
  For myself, I can only say that I was not myself,
  That day I took your war prize, the princess Briseis.
  That was not Agamemnon. That was a delusion sent

By Zeus. So now, I wish to show my true self. All
The gifts that Odysseus promised, I will make good –
And more, if you wish . . .

ACHILLES: Thank you, Agamemnon, I shall remember your words.
But today we must think of war. I shall lead the charge.
I shall be first, and with the help of Zeus,
I shall win. Follow me.

Cheers. Battle sounds

NARRATOR: Then Achilles ran to harness his horses – those famous
Horses, Firelight and Dapple-back, stronger and swifter
Than any horses in the Greek army. As Achilles
Mounted the chariot, Firelight stamped his hoof
And shook his mane, and spoke, spoke with a human voice
Which Zeus' wife, Hera, had given him.

HORSE: We shall run faster today than ever before, Achilles,
And keep you safe in the battle. But remember,
You too are a mortal man, and must die some day.

ACHILLES: Firelight, why talk of my death? I know I must die
Some day. But I shall never tire of fighting
Till I have avenged Patroklos' murder!

NARRATOR: The Trojans clustered in the centre of the plain
To await the Greek attack. Hector called out
To his soldiers.

HECTOR: Trojans, remember one thing. Achilles is only a man.
He talks loud, but I too could fight the gods
If I did it only in words.

Laughter

NARRATOR: So Hector gave his men heart, they brandished
their spears
In salute, and ran out to challenge the Greeks.
Then Achilles rode out in front, and charged
The line of spearsmen, and he was like raging
Forest fire that flares through mountain glades
Under the whip of a sharp east wind. He hacked down
Soldiers with his sword, like a reaper cutting corn.
The earth went dark with blood, and his two horses
Trampled a path over corpses and abandoned shields.
The axles and wheels of his chariot were spattered
With blood, but they did not stop, they plunged on
And on till they reached the river that runs through
The plain of Troy and is called Scamander.

There the Trojan army split in half. One part
Turned and made for the city. The other ran
Helter skelter into the swirling eddies of the river.
Once in the water they swam hither and thither

Wriggling through the fast-flowing stream
To escape Achilles. He would have slaughtered them all
Then and there, had not the river itself, taking voice,
Spoken angrily to him.

SCAMANDER: Achilles, no one can stand and resist you. You pile
Carcase upon carcase in my fresh waters, and the crush
Of bodies is choking my streams. Stop *now*!

ACHILLES: I will stop, River Scamander, when I reach
The city of Troy and kill Hector – or am killed
By him.

NARRATOR: And Achilles went on slashing and stabbing, the dead
Piled up, and he waded into the river itself.
Then the Scamander, hunching its waters together,
Whirled them like a boiling cauldron, and tossed
The bodies back on to the banks. A fearsome wave
Mounted, and curled round the head of Achilles,
And battered his shield. He could not stand upright,
And turned to reach dry ground. He was afraid.
The angry river piled itself up into a crested wave
That glowered darkly, and flung itself straight
At Achilles. He turned and ran, swift as a falcon,
The swiftest of birds, with a clatter and flash
Of armour. But the water was faster,
And wherever Achilles turned, there the river was,
Gurgling and racing towards him, its waters aswarm
With blood and bodies and armour. Had not the fire god,
Hephaistos, scooped a scorching flame from the depths
Of the earth and sent it roaring across the plain,
Achilles might have been drowned. But the river
Shrunk back before the immortal fire, and its water boiled,
Cooking the fishes and eels that swam in its eddies.
The Scamander shrivelled back to its usual size,
And Achilles was saved.

By now the rest of the Trojans had taken refuge
Inside the city walls. None of them dared to stand
In the open and face Achilles – none, except Hector.
He alone stayed outside the great west gate,
The Skaian Gate, watching Achilles race like a meteor
Across the plain.
Hector's old father, Priam, called to his son from the walls:

PRIAM: Hector, don't try to fight Achilles!
The gods protect him. I have lost too many sons
In this war.

HECTOR: I must fight him, father.

PRIAM: Please listen to me, my child, think of my grief

If you should be hurt. Stay inside the walls,
Where you're safe ... stay ... please stay ...

NARRATOR: But Hector had decided. He waited for Achilles,
Who was hurtling across the plain towards him,
Seeming to grow more huge the closer he came.
Hector did not flinch. He stood there, his shield
Planted like a tower of bronze before him,
But in his heart he was sad, thinking ...

HECTOR: I could drop my shield here, lean
My spear against the wall, and go out to meet him
Unarmed. And I could offer to give back Helen
And all the treasure she brought to Troy –
But would he listen to me? Or would he just butcher me
On the spot? ... No, this is no time for sweet talk,
Like a girl and boy meeting under a tree. This
Is a time for war, and I must fight him. So let us see
Who will be victor today.

NARRATOR: Nearer and nearer came Achilles, like the spirit
Of war incarnate, his helmet flashing, shaking
An ashwood spear in his hand. His whole body
Glittered in his armour, like a burning flame, or the sun
As it rises ... Hector trembled. He could not look
On that sight. He turned and ran!
And Achilles, like a bird of prey, raced after him,
Determined to catch him.

Round the walls of Troy they sped, past the wells
Of crystal-bright water, where the women
Used to wash their clothes in times of peace,
Before the Greek soldiers came – round and round
The walls – the one who fled was a good brave man
But the one behind was better.
And this was a race, not for the prizes that athletes win,
But for the life of Hector himself.

So Hector ran for his life, but he could not shake off
Achilles, whose feet could outrun the wind.
Whenever he tried to make for the shelter of the city walls,
Where the men on the battlements could help him
By shooting their arrows, there would be Achilles
Again, heading him off towards the open plain.
It was like a dream, in which the one who pursues
Cannot catch the one who is running in front, and the one
Who is running in front cannot ever escape his pursuer.

Three times Hector and Achilles circled the walls
Of Troy, but as Hector came to the Skaian Gate

For the fourth time, he felt ashamed, and he stopped.
He faced Achilles, and hailed him.

HECTOR: Achilles, let us make a bargain. I'll fight you
For your armour, and if I win . . .

ACHILLES: Don't bargain with me, Hector! Between men
And animals there are no bargains. They are
Eternally at war. You killed my friend Patroklos.
Now you will pay for it!

NARRATOR: As he spoke, Achilles hurled his spear, but Hector
Watched it carefully and ducked. The spear flew
Over his head and stuck in the ground. Then Hector
Threw his lance and found his mark; the point
Thudded straight into the centre of the shield
Of Achilles. But instead of driving through to the flesh
There was a clang, and the spear fell back, blunted.
Hector was angry. Now he had lost one of his weapons,
And no-one was near to hand him another. He drew
His sharp sword, and like an eagle that stoops
Through the thick clouds from high above the earth,
So Hector rushed onwards brandishing his sword.
Achilles grimly covered his body with his shield
And waited for Hector's charge, searching his frame
For a place to strike, a place where the armour left
Bare skin, and a man could be hurt. He found one –
At the base of the neck, and it was at this spot
That Achilles lunged. He moved so fast that his
Sword was a lightning stroke, and before Hector
Could ward it off the point had gashed his tender flesh,
And gone right through his neck. Hector let out
A scream and crashed to the ground . . .

HECTOR: *Gasping* Achilles, with my dying breath, I beg you,
By your life, your parents – don't leave my body
To rot out here. I have much gold and silver at home
Which my father will give you, if only you let him
Take my body away . . .

ACHILLES: Don't whine at me, dog! For the things you've done
I could eat your flesh raw!

HECTOR: I am dying, and I know your heart is made of steel.
But think of the day when my brother Paris . . .
With Apollo's help . . . Skaian . . . Gate . . .

ACHILLES: Hector! What do you mean? What will he do . . .?

NARRATOR: But Hector was dead. His spirit fled lamenting
Down to Hades, leaving his young brave body
Lying there. Achilles got no answer to his question.
Then he took two leather thongs, pierced Hector's heels,
Between the tendon and the anklebone, and threaded

The leather through. He tied the other end of the thongs
To his chariot rail, leaving the head to trail
In the dust. He mounted his chariot, lashed on
His horses, and drove round the citadel of Troy
So that everyone could see the hero Hector being dragged
Across the plain that once he ruled, his hair dulled
By dust and his handsome head all battered.
His father Priam and his mother Hecuba wept
In agony to see it. Then Achilles sent his horses
Galloping back towards the Greek ships, where the body
Of Patroklos lay on a huge pile of timber,
Whole trees laced together to make a gigantic
Funeral pyre.

ACHILLES: You men, unharness the horses . . . Now Hector . . .
We'll unharness you, and put you . . . here,
Near to Patroklos . . . where you deserve to be –
Face down in the dust and dirt!
Greek soldiers, my friends, here lies Patroklos
And here . . . lies his murderer, Hector the Trojan!
Light the fire!

NARRATOR: With Achilles leading them, they lighted torches
And filed in procession past the mound of dry wood
On which Patroklos was lying. Achilles thrust
His torch into the tinder, the other mourners
Did the same, the fire blazed high, and the Greeks
Backed away before the fierce heat. Only Achilles
Stayed, watching the flames until they died and nothing
Was left but a heap of blackened ashes.
Then he went far away by himself, along the sand,
Where the waves crashed endlessly, and walked up and down
The shore of the clamouring sea in the darkness,
Mourning for Patroklos.
At last he went back to his tent, and tried
To sleep, but sleep would not come. He lay, twisting
From side to side until, just before dawn, in the darkest,
Stillest part of the night, he heard a sound.
Footsteps. Someone had got past the guards,
And whoever it was came stealthily, not knowing the way.
Achilles leaped to his feet, and snatched up a sword.

PRIAM: *Muffled, distant* Achilles . . .?

ACHILLES: Who are you?

PRIAM: Let me in . . .

ACHILLES: Let me see your face.

PRIAM: Am I safe?

ACHILLES: Who *are* you?
    Pause

PRIAM: I am the father of Hector, king Priam of Troy . . .
　　Don't kill me, Achilles!
ACHILLES: How did you find my tent? It's dark. The camp
　　Is guarded.
PRIAM: Achilles, listen to me. I have not much time.
　　I got here because the gods took pity on me, and sent
　　A cloud of darkness to be my cloak as I came
　　Through your camp.
　　Before the sun leaves the horizon I must leave
　　Your tent, or be discovered and killed.
ACHILLES: Sit down, King Priam. Though I fight your country,
　　I know you are a brave and noble king. Sit down,
　　And drink my wine . . .
PRIAM: Thank you, Achilles . . .
　　　　　Wine is poured
　　Achilles,
　　You are as young as my own sons, and I am as old
　　As your own father. Like me, your father sits
　　In a far country, no one to protect him, alone.
　　No doubt he took great joy in you when you were there . . .
ACHILLES: Why have you come, Priam?
PRIAM: Do you pity your father, as old and helpless as I am . . . ?
ACHILLES: Yes, I do. I have often wished . . .
　　　　　Pause
PRIAM: Wished what?
ACHILLES: That I could go home and see him again.
PRIAM: So the great Achilles, tired of war, wants to go home.
ACHILLES: You still refuse to tell me what you want!
PRIAM: I want my son.
ACHILLES: Hector!
PRIAM: I want him back.
ACHILLES: He's dead, and his body belongs to me.
PRIAM: I saw what you did to his body.
ACHILLES: Did you see what he did to my friend?
PRIAM: It was done in fair fight.
ACHILLES: And I took my revenge fairly.
PRIAM: You took his life. Must you take his body too?
ACHILLES: So you've come to beg from me.
PRIAM: No, not to beg. Outside you'll find treasure
　　Enough to ransom ten king's sons.
ACHILLES: What if I say nothing can make me give up
　　My revenge . . . ?
PRIAM: I would ask you to think of your own father.
　　What would he think if he lost a son? What
　　Would he think if he knew that the son was not
　　To be buried . . . ?

ACHILLES: King Priam I . . . ! *Pause* Take your son.
NARRATOR: Achilles gave orders for Hector's body to be washed
  And covered with silks. Priam put him in a carriage
  And left the camp of the Greeks, bringing his son
  Home for the last time to Troy, where for ten days
  His countrymen mourned him.
  For each one of those days Achilles proclaimed a truce.
  Though Hector was his enemy, Achilles knew he was
  The greatest hero in the city of Troy, and he too
  Could feel sorrow at his death.

ILIAD

V The Wooden Horse

CAST:
Narrator
Apollo, god of the sun

Greeks
Agamemnon, their leader
Achilles
Odysseus
Epeios, a carpenter
Sinon
Menelaus, Helen's husband
Helen

Trojans
Priam, king of Troy
Paris, his son
Andromache, Hector's widow
Guard
1st Trojan
2nd Trojan

NARRATOR: For ten days, while Hector was buried, and the whole
  Of Troy mourned for him, there was a truce between
  The Greeks and the Trojans. But on the eleventh day
  The sentries on the battlements looked down to see
  A chariot streaking across the plain in a cloud
  Of dust. The chariot was driven by Achilles, who burned
  With battle thirst. As they looked down and saw
  His fierce eyes glaring up at them the sentries knew
  That the first man to fight Achilles in the open plain
  Would be the first to die.

  In his room in the palace, the son of Priam
  Who had lured Helen away from Greece, Paris,
  Stayed awake, day and night, trying to think
  Of a way to fight Achilles, and survive.

  It was past midnight, and the city was quiet, when he saw
  A light creep under his door from the corridor
  Outside. The light grew stronger, till it was too bright
  To look at, and flooded his whole room. The door
  Opened, and Paris covered his eyes. In the room
  Before him, in human shape, stood the sun-god himself,
  Apollo . . .

APOLLO: Look at me, Paris.

PARIS: I daren't . . . the light!

APOLLO: Then I'll make the light less. . . . Can you
  Face me now?

PARIS: It still hurts, but it's easier . . .

APOLLO: If you cannot look, Paris, then at least listen.
  You must go out and fight Achilles.

PARIS: And condemn myself to death? Achilles is immortal.

APOLLO: No man is immortal, and Achilles is a man.
  Let me tell you his secret. When he was born
  His mother, Thetis, wished her son to be
  The greatest warrior on earth. She took the baby
  And plunged him in the waters of the River Styx,
  The river of the underworld. Wherever they bathed
  His skin those waters protect it, and no weapons
  Can hurt him. But when she dipped him in the Styx,
  His mother held Achilles by his right ankle, and where
  Her hand covered his heel, there the streams
  Of the river did not touch him. That is the one
  Place where he can be hurt – his heel – and once
  The skin is pierced nothing can stop the bleeding.
  He will die.

PARIS: So long as he faces his enemies, then, they cannot
  Kill him.

APOLLO: Yes. He can only be hurt if he turns and runs.
  And that, of course, Achilles will never do.
PARIS: How can I kill him then? He will never run from me . . .
NARRATOR: But Paris was in darkness again, Apollo had gone,
  Paris was left to think about Achilles' secret,
  And when dawn came he had an idea. He went out to find
  King Rhesos, one of the allies of Troy, who was fighting
  For them against the Greeks. When he had talked to him,
  Paris set up a target in the broad main square,
  Shaped like a man, and practised his archery.

  Meanwhile, Andromache, still dressed in black
  For Hector, came to visit Helen . . .
ANDROMACHE: I saw your husband, Helen, aiming at a target.
  He missed, and hit the foot.
HELEN: Have you suddenly become an expert on war,
  Andromache?
ANDROMACHE: Enough to know that Hector is dead,
    and I·don't see
  Paris taking vengeance.
HELEN: Paris will take vengeance.
ANDROMACHE: So long as he doesn't have to take risks as well.
HELEN: Some risks are stupid, like fighting Achilles alone.
ANDROMACHE: Hector was an example – more Trojans should
    follow it.
HELEN: More Trojans should learn to be clever, like the Greeks.
ANDROMACHE: Since you admire the Greeks so much, why not
  Go back to them, Helen?
HELEN: I love Paris.
ANDROMACHE: I loved Hector. I had to part with him.
HELEN: If you had loved him more you would not have let him
  Go out to fight.
ANDROMACHE: Some men would rather serve their country
  Than a woman . . . I call them real men.
HELEN: The trouble is, most of them are dead.
      Distant roar of crowd
ANDROMACHE: What's that?
HELEN: *Moving away* Look, they're opening the gates.
ANDROMACHE: The army's going out again.
HELEN: Where's Paris? Can you see Paris?
ANDROMACHE: No . . . As usual when there's fighting to be done
  He disappears.

NARRATOR: The Trojan cavalry went out beyond the gates of Troy,
  And there stood the greatest horses in the world,
  The team owned by King Rhesos of Macedonia.
  They were all white, whiter than snow, and could

Outrun the wind – there were no horses so fine
In either army. Achilles saw them from afar, and raced out
To challenge King Rhesos and his chariot team.
Rhesos lashed his white horses into a gallop,
And they charged across the plain, their legs flashing
So fast they made a blur beneath the harness.
Achilles followed. But even Achilles,
Who could run faster than any chariot in the Greek army,
Even Achilles could not overtake those horses.
But he refused to give up. He could not bear to lose,
Lose a prize, or a race, or a battle. But he was soon
To lose his life.

King Rhesos cunningly kept his horses just ahead
Of Achilles, drawing him closer, always closer.
To Troy. There, at the Skaian Gate, out of sight,
Stood Paris, an arrow ready in his bow. He watched
The way Achilles ran, watched every movement, and as
He came closer in his wild pursuit, Paris raised
The bow. First the chariot driven by Rhesos
Hurtled past; then came Achilles, running tirelessly
To catch it. Paris let the chariot go by. As Achilles
Followed, he waited till the backs of Achilles' legs
Showed in full view, then he uttered a prayer
To Apollo, and let the arrow go. Apollo heard
The prayer and guided the arrow. It struck Achilles
Full in the heel of his right leg.

Achilles felt the blow no more than he would a thorn
From a thistle, and he kept on running. But as he went
Round the walls of Troy the chariot of King Rhesos
Seemed to pull further and further ahead . . . It hurt
Achilles to draw breath, and it appeared to him
That there was a mist on the plain of Troy – although
It was a clear sunny day. But the mist was in his eyes.
He looked behind him and saw, in his own tracks,
Blood, saw the broken arrow, with its point still
In his heel, and felt the warm blood flowing,
Flowing from that little wound . . . By now he was back
Once more at the Skaian Gate, where Paris had first
Shot his arrow. Achilles knelt in the dust. He felt
His strength going. He looked up and saw Paris,
Still with the bow in his hand.

ACHILLES: *Hoarsely* So handsome . . . so cunning . . . you hide
  In the shadows, Paris . . . perfect . . . Woman chaser!
  With your bow and arrow – coward's weapons . . .!
PARIS: No, Achilles, I won because

Apollo wants Troy to be safe. You'll die for nothing,
Achilles, because you Greeks will never take Troy!
NARRATOR: There was no reply from Achilles. He sank back
In the dust, while over the plain towards him came
A cloud of sea-spray, blown in from the ocean.
Before the Trojans could run out from their city
And snatch up his body, that sea-mist rolled over
Achilles, hiding him from sight, and stinging
Their eyes, so that they could see nothing.
When the mist cleared Achilles' body, and the beautiful armour
Forged by Hephaistos, had all vanished. The mist
Had been sent by his mother, Thetis, who now
Reclaimed her son and bore him far below the waves
To be buried in a sea-cave of cold and glittering jewels.
While he lived, Achilles was the greatest warrior
And noblest king the Greeks had ever known.
None who came after him was so brave, and his name
Was remembered for all time. Zeus kept his promise.
Though Achilles' life was short, his fame
Was everlasting.

Achilles was dead, and now the Greeks despaired.
They thought the war was lost. Only Odysseus
Refused to give up hope, and one morning he came
To Agamemnon, bringing a short wrinkled man with him.
ODYSSEUS: Agamemnon, let me introduce Epeios.
AGAMEMNON: Who is he?
ODYSSEUS: A carpenter. A good carpenter . . .
AGAMEMNON: We shall need him. We have many ships to repair
Before we set sail for home.
ODYSSEUS: Not yet, Agamemnon. Don't talk of sailing home
Till you've heard the brilliant ideas of my friend
Epeios . . . Epeios – talk brilliantly!
EPEIOS: *Stammering nervously* Well, sir . . . I . . . you see . . .
ODYSSEUS: He's a little shy, Agamemnon, you must excuse him . . .
Come on, Epeios, courage! Talk like the genius you are!
EPEIOS: *After a struggle* It's a horse. *Pause*
ODYSSEUS: You see, Agamemnon?
AGAMEMNON: Odysseus, he may be good at carpentry, but with
words
He doesn't exactly hit the nail on the head.
ODYSSEUS: He means – the trick by which we shall take
The city of Troy is contained in the idea
Of a gigantic horse . . . Right, Epeios?
EPEIOS: Right, sir, right!
AGAMEMNON: Will this plan work?

ODYSSEUS: Have any of our other plans worked?

AGAMEMNON: No.

ODYSSEUS: Then Epeios can do no worse, and might even
Do better. Trust me, Agamemnon.

NARRATOR: Agamemnon had no choice, and Epeios was given
All the wood he asked for. Behind a tall screen
Of wicker and canvas he worked in secret for forty
Days and nights, hammering and sawing, planing
And chiselling. Then, one evening, it was all silent.

The Trojan watchmen, spying on the Greek camp,
Saw a flame flicker up, then another, then another . . .
And soon the entire Greek camp was ablaze.
For most of the night the fire raged, and when morning
Came the Trojans stood in amazement on their city walls
Looking at the place where the Greek army had been.
All the tents, the stockades for the horses, the ramparts,
The workshops – everything was burnt to the ground.
And the ships were gone. Only one thing remained.
Half way between the sea and the walls of Troy,
In the centre of the plain, stood a wooden horse.
Three houses piled on top of each other would not
Have reached to the crest of its mane, and each
Of its wooden legs was as thick as a pillar
In the temple of Olympian Zeus.

King Priam called a meeting of his council.
They had all seen the wooden horse, but no-one
Could decide what should be done with it.

PARIS: Father, let me speak . . .

PRIAM: Yes, Paris?

PARIS: Father, whatever this object, this horse, may be,
One thing I know for sure. It's dangerous.
        Reaction
I know, you think I'm too cautious, but I prefer
To be a live coward than a dead fool.

GUARD: *Approaching* My Lords . . . King Priam! . . . I did it!

PRIAM: Did what? You should be on duty. All sentries
Are to remain at their posts . . .

GUARD: But my lord, I captured him, all by myself.
I hope there's a reward. If there is,
I get it all!

PRIAM: Captured whom?

GUARD: Some Greek! He's been
Left behind by the fleet.

PRIAM: Where is he?

GUARD: Just outside . . . Bring in the prisoner!

Footsteps approaching, clink of chains
Here he is. Not much to look at, but I did
Do it all alone . . . He says his name is Sinon.
SINON: Correct. But don't call me Greek. I hate
All Greeks, and from now on I want to forget
I was born one myself.
PARIS: Why? What happened?
SINON: I was a friend of Palamedes, a great lord
In the Greek army, and the treacherous, black-hearted
Scum, Odysseus, killed him! I want revenge for that!
PRIAM: Then why didn't you sail with the fleet and take it?
SINON: I wanted to help you because that will hurt them
Most. Listen, do you want to know the secret
Of the wooden horse . . . ?
Reaction
Then I'll tell you. That horse is an offering
To the goddess Athene. They built it to bring them
Good luck on their voyage home.
PRIAM: They've gone home?
SINON: Yes. *Relief from his audience* Wait, there's more.
They built the horse so big, to make sure
It could not get through the gates of Troy.
They were afraid, you see, that you might drag it
Into the city, and so the good luck would leave them
And go to you.
PRIAM: There's a simple answer to that. We'll just lift
The top off the Skaian Gate . . . Paris, collect
Some men and start to pull the horse this way . . .
NARRATOR: While Priam's Trojans laboured to lift
The topmost arch off the city gate, the strongest
Soldiers went out with Paris, taking ropes
And chains and teams of oxen, to haul the great horse
Up to the city. Logs were placed under it, and slowly
It began to roll across the plain.
Inside the horse: hollow rumbling echo
ODYSSEUS: We're moving.
MENELAUS: At last. I hope not into the sea, Odysseus.
ODYSSEUS: No, Menelaus. Uphill. Towards Troy.
Bump. Curses
Quiet, you men back there!
MENELAUS: When Epeios designed this horse I wish he'd considered
The comfort of the people who have to ride in it.
ODYSSEUS: Patience, Menelaus. Would you rather be on board
Your ship, being seasick?
A specially loud bump, groans
MENELAUS: Frankly – yes!

NARRATOR: Groaning and creaking, the horse lumbered over
　　The rocky ground, through the gates, along the streets,
　　Till it stopped in the main square of Troy.
　　Men, women and children filled the streets,
　　Dancing in a carnival of joy. The war was over,
　　They had stolen the wooden horse, and all their sorrows
　　Were forgotten. That night was a festival, with songs
　　And dances, wine, and flute-music sounding
　　Throughout the city.
　　　　　Muffled sounds of music and dancing,
　　　　　as if heard through a wall. When the characters speak, there is
　　　　　some echo, as if in a small enclosed space
MENELAUS: Odysseus?
ODYSSEUS: *Sleepily* Yes, Menelaus?
MENELAUS: Are you asleep?
ODYSSEUS: I was.
MENELAUS: My nose tickles.
ODYSSEUS: Scratch it.
MENELAUS: Inside. It tickles inside. I'm going to sneeze.
ODYSSEUS: *Wide awake* Ssh! There are guards all around
　　The horse, my lord Menelaus. They'll hear you!
MENELAUS: I can't help it. I'm going to sneeze.
ODYSSEUS: Blow your nose, and see if that helps.
　　　　　Snort
　　How do you feel?
　　　　　Pause
MENELAUS: It still tickles.
ODYSSEUS: By Zeus and all the gods on Olympus, you can't
　　Give away our secret *now*! We'll all be killed!
MENELAUS: I'm sorry, Odysseus . . . aah . . . aah . . .
ODYSSEUS: Get your swords out, men!
　　　　　They draw their swords
MENELAUS: It's coming . . .
ODYSSEUS: Sell your lives dearly, men!
MENELAUS: I'm going . . . to . . . sneeze . . . now . . .
ODYSSEUS: Ready?
　　　　　Murmurs from men, noise of music and dancing suddenly
　　　　　very loud. We are outside the horse. Muffled, but distinct,
　　　　　comes the sound of an almighty sneeze
1st TROJAN: Did you hear that?
2nd TROJAN: The horse spoke . . .
1st TROJAN: A sign from Olympos.
2nd TROJAN: Fortune is with us.
1st TROJAN: Praise the goddess Athene!
2nd TROJAN: Praise . . . *Hic* . . . Athene . . . *Drunken snore*
NARRATOR: One by one the happy Trojans

Fell asleep, until the only sound to be heard
Was the snoring of the guards, slumped over their shields
On the battlements.

The rays of the moon silvered the wooden horse
In the square, and if there had been a single Trojan
Awake he would have seen Sinon, the captured Greek,
Steal across to the horse and open a small trap door
In its belly. Through the opening a foot appeared.
The foot belonged to Odysseus. Then followed
Menelaus, and Ajax, and after them, a picked band
Of the fiercest Greek warriors.

Meanwhile, the Greek fleet was only a few miles
Off shore, and rowing back as fast it could under cover
Of night.

Through the moonlit sleeping streets the soldiers
Crept towards the palace, and surrounded it. Then
They killed the sleeping sentries at the gates,
And when dawn came the Trojans awoke to find
Their homeland captured. They ran to take up arms.
Some snatched knives and clubs, others picked up
Stones or built barricades. But everywhere they went
They were met by well-armed Greeks, who spared no-one.
The Greek ships were beached once more. The city
Gates were opened, and the main Greek army marched
Through the streets. Then plunder and murder began,
All Troy's treasure was ransacked, temples of gods
Destroyed, the women and children enslaved,
The best of the warriors killed. When the Greeks
Had finished, Troy was a heap of smouldering ruins,
And the fleet sailed away, laden with all the riches
That once had graced Priam's famous city. Never again
Would Troy rise in glory on the shores of the eastern sea.
The Greeks had taken everything, and Menelaus
Had won his Helen back.

ODYSSEY

ODYSSEY

I The Cyclops

CAST:

Narrator
Odysseus
Lotos Eater
1st Sailor
2nd Sailor
3rd Sailor
4th Sailor
Cyclops
1st Cyclops
2nd Cyclops
3rd Cyclops

NARRATOR: Troy was in ruins. The high walls lay shattered.
  The Greeks had looted the treasuries, enslaved the women, and now
  They launched their ships, laden with spoil, and scattered
  For home.
  In one of these ships sailed Odysseus, King of Ithaca.
  Odysseus was famous for his brainful of tricks – famous
  On earth, where no-one could match his cunning – famous
  In heaven too.
  The ship was ready and Odysseus shouted:

ODYSSEUS: Hoist the sails, men, the wind's in our favour.
  Helmsman, set course for Ithaca, we're going home.
  Do you hear that, men? After ten years of war
  We're on our way home!
          Cheers

NARRATOR: Nine days they sailed, but all nine days the winds
  Blew against them, and on the tenth they were driven to land,
  The country of the Lotos Eaters.
  They went ashore to take on fresh water, and Odysseus chose
  Three men to go and explore. Now the Lotos Eaters
  Live on flowers, flowers are their only food,
  And they welcomed Odysseus' men with a meal of Lotos blooms.
  They meant to be kind when they gave the men a meal
  Of those sweet honey-dew flowers. But the worst of the Lotos,
  Its lure and deceit, lies in its strange, its lasting,
  Its clinging embrace. From the very first taste the men
  Wanted more, then more, then still more.

1st SAILOR: More – more, please . . . it's like food the gods might
    eat.

2nd SAILOR: It makes you feel . . . free, free of everything.
          Pause

2nd SAILOR: *Dreamily* How long have we been here?

LOTOS EATER: Why ask? We don't count time in Lotos Land.

1st SAILOR: What do you work at?

LOTOS EATER: The world's work is a senseless game. Here we have
    all
  We need in the Lotos flower.

NARRATOR: The hours passed, they never noticed them. But
    Odysseus,
  Waiting at the ship, grew restless and angry, and at last
  Set out in search of his men. He found them surrounded
  By Lotos blossoms, smiling, uncaring.

ODYSSEUS: You! . . . Why are you sitting there?
  I told you to report back to the ship!

1st SAILOR: Taste this flower, Odysseus.

ODYSSEUS: I've eaten. Come back to the ship.

1st SAILOR: What for?

ODYSSEUS: What for? To go home, of course.

1st SAILOR: Who cares about home? We have Lotos petals to eat.

ODYSSEUS: What about your wife? Your children?

2nd SAILOR: Who cares about wives?

LOTOS EATER: Odysseus, eat a Lotos flower . . .

ODYSSEUS: No! No! Friends, think of your house,
Your work . . .

1st SAILOR: House – a waste of time. Work – a stupid game.
Compared with Lotos petals, nothing matters.
When I eat them, I see such beautiful things, dream
Such beautiful dreams.

2nd SAILOR: I want just to pluck them and eat them, eat them and
dream. . . .

ODYSSEUS: You have your orders!
He draws his sword

Get up!

SAILORS: No, Odysseus, no, no, no, . . .

NARRATOR: Odysseus had to haul them back
By force. They hated to go, struggled against him, but he
Put them in irons in the hold of his ship, and ordered
His crew to hurry, quickly, back on board, set sail,
Before anyone else tasted a Lotos flower, and forgot
They were bound for home. The crew ran to their places,
Sat on the benches, snatched up their oars, and churned
The sea to white foam as they went.

On they sailed, fear in their hearts – but still they went on.
Land appeared once more – Cyclops country. Here lived giants,
Monsters with only one eye in the centre of their heads.
Their homes were great caverns in the hill sides,
Where they lived alone, without law or love for each other.
Odysseus found a sheltered harbour, beached the ship,
And gave his men a chance to gather new strength for the
journey.
The air was thick and still, no moon shone that night,
Clouds pressed down and stole away sight. All around
They could hear the sound of the one-eyed giants
Moving about the fields, tending their sheep and goats.
When morning came they went out hunting, and found wild goats
In the cliffs. That day they had all the meat they could eat,
Washed down with sweet red wine – they still had some casks
Left in the ship. Then Odysseus called his crew together:

ODYSSEUS: Friends, I want to find out what kind of people live
here.
Twelve of the best men are to come with me. The rest
To stay and guard the ship.

NARRATOR: Having chosen his men, Odysseus took a flask of wine,
    Dark and red – the best they had – and left. Climbing quickly,
    They came to a cave, but found no-one there. Cyclops
    Was out with his flocks of sheep in the pastures.
    Odysseus and his men went inside and gazed at the cave.
    There were baskets crammed with cheese, stockades full
    Of lambs and kids, there was row upon row of pots
    And jugs and milking pails.

    At the sight of all this wealth the sailors begged Odysseus
    To take the cheese, drive off the lambs and kids, hurry
    Back to the ship – and set sail for the open sea.
    Odysseus said no – but later he was sorry. Cyclops
    Had a rough welcome in store for his men.
    So they lit a fire, and made free with the cheese,
    And sat there, eating and warming themselves, and waiting
    For Cyclops. At sundown he came, herding his flocks
    Of sheep. On his back he carried a tremendous load
    Of dried wood for his cooking fire, which he dropped
    On the floor of the cave with a clatter. The men
    Took fright and ran to the back, where they hid
    In the shadows. Then Cyclops heaved
    A great boulder into the entrance to block the mouth
    Of the cave. That boulder was so huge – twenty carts
    With four wheels and good strong timbers could never shift it
    From its place. Cyclops lit a fire to make his supper –
    Then he saw them.
CYCLOPS: Who are you? I don't know you! . . . Sailors, I see.
    Where from?
    Are you traders? Or are you prowling the sealanes
    Living from day to day on what you can steal? Is that
    Your trade – piracy?
NARRATOR: His voice crushed them, his huge bulk terrified them,
    And their hearts stumbled, but Odysseus replied
    To Cyclops' question:
ODYSSEUS: We are Greeks. We started from Troy, and were bound
    for home
    When we lost our way in a maze of winds and waves, and now
    We are far off course . . . Well, such is the will of Zeus.
    Can you give us shelter, help us, perhaps, do us some
    Kindness? We are travellers, it is our sacred right –
    And remember, sir, there are gods who guard these rights.
    Zeus knows what happens to every traveller. He watches over us,
    And sees us safe.
CYCLOPS: A very foolish traveller, from a very distant country,
    Who tells me, a Cyclops, to beware of gods. A Cyclops

Despises all gods. We are stronger, and greater
Than any of them!

NARRATOR: Without another word he lunged forward and his hands
Darted amongst Odysseus' men, and plucked out two,
And then, as easily as if they were two little puppies,
He smashed them on the ground. Their heads split open,
And their brains spilled out and soaked the earth.
Cyclops sliced them up and prepared his dinner.
He was like a ravening lion; he ate everything –
Flesh, innards, and bones.

Odysseus and his men, watching this cruel feast,
Lifted pleading hands to heaven in anguish. But no help
Came. They had to swallow their rage.
When Cyclops had packed his enormous stomach full
Of human flesh and draughts of fresh milk, he stretched
Out to sleep among his flocks of sheep, filling
The whole length of the cave.
Odysseus went up to him, a brave plan forming. . . .

ODYSSEUS: *In a whisper* Should I draw my sharp sword – now! I
have it ready
At my side – stab him – there, under his ribs –
I could reach his liver . . . No! Stop! Think again.
We would all die here with him, certain and slow,
Because never never could we shift with our own bare hands
That brute of a boulder he used to block the mouth
Of the cave.

NARRATOR: So Odysseus and his men, without hope, without
sleep,
Waited . . . The sky was touched with rose-pink rays
Of light, a fresh glow spread – dawn.
Cyclops lit his fire, and milked his sheep, and gave
Each one its lamb to suckle, and the day began
As it always did . . . except for one thing.
For his breakfast that day Cyclops snatched two more
Of Odysseus' men. When he had eaten them he drove
His sheep out of the cave, easily lifting
The vast stone away from the entrance – but the next
Instant he dropped it back in place like someone stopping
The mouth of a quiver. Then up to the mountains
With his sheep went Cyclops, whistling all the way.
Odysseus sat thinking – raging. He must have revenge!
At last a plan came to him – a brilliant plan, he thought.

ODYSSEUS: We'll use that.

3rd SAILOR: What? That tree trunk over there?

ODYSSEUS: Yes, Cyclops' club. We'll use that.

4th SAILOR: Use it! We couldn't even lift it. It's as big as the mast
    Of a cargo ship.

ODYSSEUS: We want about – so much – cut off it. I'll stretch
    My arms out wide. Right – now measure the distance
    From finger tip to finger tip.

3rd SAILOR: That's about six feet, sir.

ODYSSEUS: Good, take your swords, and hack that piece off.

SAILORS: With our swords?

ODYSSEUS: With your swords!
       Cutting that slows down, then a sharp crack

3rd SAILOR: There you are, sir, six feet of useless tree trunk.

ODYSSEUS: Now, make it smooth all round while I sharpen the end.

4th SAILOR: I don't see the point of this at all. Are we going to
    drill our way out?

ODYSSEUS: Cyclops will get the point . . . Make sure you leave no
    rough
    Edges. I want a nice smooth sharp stake. . . .
       Knife carving wood
    Good. Now into the fire with it, and make it hard,
    Hard as steel.
       The stake is put in the embers
    Don't let it burn, just temper it . . . Good . . . Now,
    Quickly, take it and hide it – here, under this pile
    Of dirt . . . Make sure Cyclops can't see it . . .

4th SAILOR: All done, sir.

3rd SAILOR: What do we do now?

ODYSSEUS: Wait for Cyclops.

4th SAILOR: That'll be a pleasure!

ODYSSEUS: This time we're ready for him.

NARRATOR: Evening came, and so did Cyclops, driving his sheep.
    As before, he milked them and then made his meal.
    As before, his meal was two of Odysseus' men.
    Then Odysseus got up and went to speak to him. In his hands
    Was a cup of the strong dark wine they had brought from the ship.

ODYSSEUS: Cyclops, here, drink some wine. This will show you
    What we carry in our ship. Perhaps it will make you pity us,
    And let us go home.

CYCLOPS: I like it.

ODYSSEUS: Good.

CYCLOPS: I like it tremendously.

ODYSSEUS: I'm glad.

CYCLOPS: Give me some more.

ODYSSEUS: *pouring* With pleasure.

CYCLOPS: *drinking* Tell me your name, stranger . . . More of this
    stuff!

ODYSSEUS: *pouring* My name? Why?

CYCLOPS: I want to reward you, give you something ... More, I
    said!
    Fill the cup.
ODYSSEUS: *pouring* Hold it steady ... What will you give me?
CYCLOPS: It *is* steady – d'you think I can't hold a cup ...
    I'll give you anything you like ... *drinking* More!
ODYSSEUS: My name ... careful, don't spill it ... my name,
    Cyclops,
    Is Nobody. My mother and father and all my friends
    Call me Nobody.
CYCLOPS: Good. Then here ... *drinks* ... is the reward ...
    hic ... I promised you, Nobody. You shall be saved ... *drinks*
    ... till I have finished your friends. I shall eat you ...
    hic ... last of all! ... I'm so generous ... *hic*, ha ha. ...
    ... I'm so generous I can't stand myself!
        Hiccups to laughter to snoring ...

NARRATOR: He lay down to sleep and keeled over on his back.
    His neck flopped to one side, his mouth slobbered wine
    And chunks of human flesh. He was sodden and belching,
    Sunk in a drunken sleep.

    Odysseus took the sharpened stake from its hiding place,
    Held it deep in the embers of the fire, and let it grow warm,
    Talking to his men all the time to keep their courage alive,
    And not fail him now. Soon the olive wood, green though it was,
    Began to glow fiercely. Just as it was about to catch fire
    Odysseus snatched it from the embers. Now was the moment.
    His men sprang to their places – prayed for strength –
    Seized the stake – and ground it deep into Cyclops' one
    And only eye.
    Cyclops let out a horrible shriek, the rock walls rang
    And clamoured, the sailors scattered in fear. Cyclops
    Wrenched out the stake spattered with gouts of blood from
        his eye
    And threw it in agony far away from him. Then he screamed
    For help from his giant neighbours. They heard his noise
    And came running from all directions. They gathered round
    The entrance to his cave:
1st CYCLOPS: What's happening?
2nd CYCLOPS: What did you wake us for?
3rd CYCLOPS: Is someone stealing your sheep?
1st CYCLOPS: Is someone killing you?
CYCLOPS: Nobody's killing me! Nobody!
1st CYCLOPS: If no-one's killing you there's no help on earth for
    you.
2nd CYCLOPS: Pray to heaven to make you sane again.

NARRATOR: And they left him.
   All this time Odysseus was laughing to himself, while Cyclops,
   Moaning and gasping in pain, groped his way to the front
   Of the cave, and shifted the boulder from its place.
   He posted himself in the entrance, spreading wide
   His arms to catch the men as they slipped out past him.
   But Odysseus was not so foolish as that. He was thinking
   How to save himself and his men. Life was at stake,
   The danger great, and he had many ideas. He tried them all
   In his mind, till one seemed best.

   Cyclops' sheep were huge fat beasts, with fleeces
   Sweeping down in long curls. Now Odysseus harnessed them
   Together in threes, side by side; the middle one
   Carried a man slung beneath, the other two helped to cover
   And shield him. Three sheep, then, for every man.
   For himself, Odysseus picked the leader of the flock,
   A strong giant of a ram, and hung under his belly,
   Curled up in the curtains of thick wool. They waited . . .

   Dawn came, filling the sky with rose, and Cyclops
   Began to drive his flocks out to pasture.
   Racked with pain he stood, feeling the backs of the sheep
   As they trotted past. But the great fool never thought
   The men might be fastened beneath, hidden in the fleece.
   Last of all came the ram who was the leader of the flock,
   Carrying, besides the weight of its own heavy coat,
   Odysseus, praying his plan would work.
   Cyclops checked the ram, passed his hands all over it,
   Mumbled . . .
CYCLOPS: Why last of all . . .? My best ram, last to leave the cave.
   Always used to lead the way, always went running first
   For the long grass and the sweet flowers . . . Are you sorry
   For your master? Do you pity his one blind eye?
NARRATOR: Then he pushed the ram away from him.
   Out of the cave – out of the darkness – out of Cyclops'
   Power! . . . Quickly Odysseus untied himself, and helped
   His sailors free.
ODYSSEUS: Hurry – fast as you can, round up the sheep!
     Sheep noises, shouting from the men
4th SAILOR: Good sheep, aren't they – fat and meaty . . .
3rd SAILOR: Think of it. Fresh mutton for the rest of the voyage.
ODYSSEUS: Down to the ship, quick, before Cyclops hears us . . .
     Fade to sea shore, beach sounds
1st SAILOR: Look! . . . It's Odysseus, and the others – they're
   driving
   A flock of sheep.

2nd SAILOR: Safe! They're all safe.

1st SAILOR: Not all. Count again . . .

ODYSSEUS: *far off* Be ready to sail. We leave now! . . .
> *The men cheer*

3rd and 4th SAILORS: *approaching* Quick . . . on board . . . hurry now . . . get
Those sheep on board.
> *More cheers, shouts, sheep noises, then roar of Cyclops*

CYCLOPS: Stop! . . . STOP! . . .

ODYSSEUS: Quiet, men, get the ship under way – don't let him
Hear us!

CYCLOPS: *closer* My sheep! Someone's stolen my sheep!

SAILORS: *lowered voices* All aboard, sir, ready to sail now . . .

ODYSSEUS: Make for the open sea . . .
> *Ship noises, creaking timbers, rowing*

CYCLOPS: Thieves! Stop! Stop!

ODYSSEUS: Hurry – or we're lost! . . .

NARRATOR: They leapt to their places, sat on the benches
And in quick succession, one, two, three, clashed their oars
In the waves . . . The shore was shouting distance behind them
When Odysseus started to hurl insults back at Cyclops.

ODYSSEUS: You thought you'd a poor weak man at your mercy.
You thought you'd bully him, terrorise him, eat him!
Butcher! Cannibal! Zeus has punished you now!

NARRATOR: Cyclops, foaming with rage, wrenched the top off a mountain,
And hurled it at the ship. It fell just a little in front
Of the bow.
> *Splash of rock in sea*
The sea boiled up as the mass of rock descended,
Washing the ship on a tidal wave back to the shore.

ODYSSEUS: *above roars of water* Row! Row!

1st SAILOR: We're going to run aground!

ODYSSEUS: Give me that pole – here . . . Push, help me . . .

4th SAILOR: It's no good, sir, the wave's too strong!

ODYSSEUS: Row hard – harder! Push her off into deep water . . .
Harder!
> *Sounds of rowing, grunts, straining*
Goodbye, Cyclops – thank you for the sheep.

3rd SAILOR: *out of breath* Don't, sir, please don't . . . he'll
Hear you!

ODYSSEUS: *bolder* Back to your cave, Cyclops, your man-meals
Are finished.

2nd SAILOR: In the name of heaven, sir, don't bait him!

ODYSSEUS: It's all right, we're safe out here.

CYCLOPS: Nobody! I'll kill you, Nobody, I'll kill you! . . .

ODYSSEUS: Wrong again, Cyclops. I'm somebody. If anyone asks
you
Who took away your eye, tell them it was Odysseus –
Odysseus, destroyer of cities and sight!
CYCLOPS: Odysseus! Now I understand. Now the old prophecy
Comes true. I was warned once by a fortune teller
That a man called Odysseus would come to destroy me.
But I was looking for a mighty warrior, a strong great hero.
You are a little runt, useless and weak – and you blinded me
By making me drunk. I pray you never reach home.
And if you do I pray it costs you dear in suffering
And misery; may you arrive half dead, alone, without
Your dear comrades, and when you get there may you find
Chaos and sorrow. Poseidon, god of the sea, is my father.
I pray to Poseidon to help me, and I know he will.
NARRATOR: He heaved an even greater lump of rock out
Towards the ship, flinging it high in the air. It fell
Just short of the stern, and the sea surged beneath its weight.
The sailors rowed with all their might, till the waves
Were froth under their oars, and escaped. But they were sad
At heart. They had lost good friends, whom they loved . . .
They themselves, though, were safe – and for that
They were thankful.

ODYSSEY
II Aiolos and Circe

CAST:

NARRATOR: Sailing from Cyclops land, Odysseus and his men came
   To an island floating in the sea, and its king, Aiolos,
   Was friendly and welcomed them. For one whole month
   The sailors were his guests, while he listened to the story
   Of the war at Troy. When Odysseus had told it all
   He asked Aiolos to let them go on their way. Aiolos
   Agreed, and helped them prepare for the journey.
   On the last day he gave Odysseus a parting gift –
   The flayed hide of a nine-year-old bull. Sewn up inside
   This hide, and making it bulge, were winds – a wind
   For every way a man could sail. Aiolos had special powers
   Over winds; he could tame them, arouse them,
   Do what he liked with them. Now he twisted a silver thread
   Round the neck of the leather, to make sure not even
   A breath of wind escaped, and put the sack in the hold
   Of the ship, leaving out only a westerly breeze to speed
   The vessel and its crewmen home.

   Night and day, for nine days, they sailed,
   Until on the tenth they sighted land – home. It was so close
   They could see the watchfires burning.
   All this time Odysseus had kept the helm himself,
   Letting no-one else touch it, to make sure they reached home
   Sooner. But now he needed sleep, and gently, lovingly, sleep
   Overwhelmed him.
   Meanwhile, his crew began to talk.

1st SAILOR: He's got all this gold and silver . . .

2nd SAILOR: He's got presents from Aiolos . . .

1st SAILOR: And what have we got? Nothing! We've travelled as
   far . . .

2nd SAILOR: Yes – sailed as many miles, and we come home with
   what?

ALL: Nothing! . . .

1st SAILOR: Let's see what this present from Aiolos is . . .

2nd SAILOR: Yes, let's see how much treasure he's got in this sack!

1st SAILOR: Feels light as air.

2nd SAILOR: It must be precious, the way these cords are tied.

3rd SAILOR: Careful, don't wake Odysseus.

2nd SAILOR: Help me undo these knots . . .
      Hissing sound

1st SAILOR: Wind's getting up a bit.

2nd SAILOR: Good, we'll be home by dawn . . . That's one knot,
   now
   The next. . . .
      Louder hissing

3rd SAILOR: Never known of a wind get up so fast.

1st SAILOR: It's blowing near a gale.

3rd SAILOR: From a different quarter too . . .

2nd SAILOR: Give me your knife. I'm going to cut this cord.

3rd SAILOR: Here . . .

2nd SAILOR: Right. Now, let's see what's in this sack.

> *Brief pause, while he cuts the cord, then . . . a sudden howling gale, shrieks of wind . . .*

NARRATOR: It was a bad idea, a stupid idea, but they couldn't resist.
They opened the sack, all the winds tore out, a sudden
Storm whipped the ship out to sea, and the sailors wept
As home vanished over the horizon.

> *Storm*

The winds flung them on the island of Aiaie. They beached
Their ship, collapsed in the sand, and for two days
And nights they lay there, overcome with fatigue
And despair.
When the third day dawned Odysseus climbed the steep path
That led up from the beach, until he could see out
Over the island. There were woods, and forests – and smoke
Rising above the trees . . . He decided to explore.

Back at his ship he counted off his crew and made
Two sections. Each section had a leader – Odysseus himself
Commanded one, Eurylochos, handsome as a young god,
The other. Then they put two pebbles into a bronze helmet,
One pebble for Odysseus, one for Eurylochos, and shook
The helmet hard. Out jumped the pebble of Eurylochos.
Taking twenty-two men he set off inland, full
Of foreboding. Odysseus stayed behind with the rest,
Heavy hearted.

Deep in a wood, in the middle of a clearing, Eurylochos
And his men found a house, built of smooth stone blocks.
Circe lived there, a great and beautiful witch.
All around paced wolves and mountain lions, but they made
No move to attack. They were just like dogs fawning
On their master the way they sidled up to the men.
But the sailors were afraid when they saw those beasts
With their cruel claws and fierce eyes, and huddled
In the doorway of the beautiful witch's house.
Inside they could hear someone singing. It was Circe
Working at her loom, her great magic loom, on which
She wove cloth so fine and silky and soft to the touch.

1st SAILOR: Who is it?

2nd SAILOR: I don't know . . . What shall we do, Eurylochos?

EURYLOCHOS: Careful men, this may be a demon, or a witch.

3rd SAILOR: Sounds like a peaceful woman to me. Listen –
  She's weaving.
      Singing, sound of shuttle
EURYLOCHOS: I say we go back to the ship. I don't like the feel
  Of this place.
3rd SAILOR: Let's see her first. We've come all this way.
SAILORS: Yes, yes, call her out, see what she's like . . .
EURYLOCHOS: All right, men, but be careful . . .
1st SAILOR: You knock, then.
2nd SAILOR: No, you.
1st SAILOR: It was your idea.
3rd SAILOR: You wanted to see her too . . .
2nd SAILOR: I'll knock.
      He knocks on the door. The singing stops
1st SAILOR: *whisper* She's coming.
      Footsteps, door opens
CIRCE: Welcome, sailors. I saw your ship from far away.
  I was expecting you. Come inside, you must be tired . . .
  Come inside.
NARRATOR: Without thinking
  The men accepted, and followed her. Only Eurylochos
  Suspecting a trick, stayed behind.

  Circe took the men to a room with chairs and couches.
  She gave them wine to drink, she gave them cheese,
  And barley cake, and mixed in with all this she gave them
  A drug – an evil concoction that made them forget
  Who they were and where they came from. When they had
    drunk it
  She tapped them with her wand, and herded them all
  Into pig pens. Now they had the heads and bodies
  Of pigs, pigs' hides, and pigs' grunts – but their minds
  Were still human, they knew what was done to them, knew
  They were prisoners. Circe tossed them some acorns
  And husks and berries to eat . . .
CIRCE: . . . Proper food for pigs who sleep in the mud!
NARRATOR: Eurylochos ran headlong back to the ship, to tell
  The story of his men's weird enchantment. But when
  He arrived shock and fear gagged him. He tried to speak
  But no words came, he choked in terror, his eyes
  Brimmed with tears. The sailors kept asking him – why?
  Why? . . . and at last he found his voice and told them . . .
  As the story ended, Odysseus buckled on his great bronze sword
  With its silver studs, and ordered Eurylochos to lead him
  Back to the clearing. Eurylochos clutched at him
  And begged him not to go. His voice was shaking. . . .

EURYLOCHOS: Let me stay here, sir, please! I know you'll never
  Return! You'll never bring any of the men back either.
  Let's leave now. We're safe. Let's go while we can!
ODYSSEUS: Stay here, Eurylochos, I'll go alone. It is my duty,
  Nothing can stop me.
NARRATOR: Odysseus left them.

The ship was out of sight, the sea was behind him,
And he was just at the edge of the magic wood
Where Circe lived, when a young man met him.
He was gentle-looking, with the beginnings of a beard,
And he was really Hermes, guide and messenger of the gods,
In disguise. Hermes stopped Odysseus with a touch.
HERMES: Where are you going, you fool? You're alone, in a dark
  Wood, you don't know the way, your men are in Circe's power.
  You will never come back from Circe's house unless
  You take a charm with you. I'll give you one.
  It's strong and certain, and will guard you through
  The worst of your days.
NARRATOR: Hermes reached down and plucked a flower from the
    earth –
  It had a black root, and petals the colour of milk.
  The gods call it Moly; men find it hard to come by
  But gods can do anything.

Hermes vanished, and Odysseus went on his way.
His heart was thudding as he laid his plans.
At the doorway of the house he stopped.
        Singing, he knocks, the singing stops, footsteps, door opens
CIRCE: Welcome, sailor. I saw your ship from far away.
  I was expecting you. Come inside, you must be tired . . .
ODYSSEUS: Thank you.
CIRCE: This way . . . In my great hall a banquet is ready . . .
ODYSSEUS: You do me too much honour, my lady.
CIRCE: Nothing is too good for a guest in my house. . . . Now,
  Come and sit down. My servants will bring you
  Anything you need.
ODYSSEUS: You are so kind and generous. Surely no one who comes
  Here would ever want to leave.
CIRCE: But they do. Unfortunately, they soon go to other
  Lodgings, and other food.
ODYSSEUS: How strange, I wonder why.
CIRCE: A change seems to come over them . . . Will you have
  Something to drink?
ODYSSEUS: Thank you, yes.
CIRCE: Good. You must be very thirsty . . .
        Glass tinkles

I'll give you this and you'll feel a different person.
ODYSSEUS: What do you put in it?
CIRCE: That's a secret, but it will do wonders for you.
            Pouring
ODYSSEUS: *To himself* And *to* me, you hope.
CIRCE: What did you say?
ODYSSEUS: I was saying, it looks good.
CIRCE: Why don't you drink?
ODYSSEUS: Why are you watching me?
CIRCE: To see if you like it.
ODYSSEUS: My first drink is a toast to you.
CIRCE: Thank you, stranger, good health.
            Odysseus drinks
    What do you feel?
ODYSSEUS: What you wished me – good health.
CIRCE: Let me touch you once with my wand and we'll see . . .
    Now! To the pigsty. Go and wallow with your friends!
ODYSSEUS: No, Circe! Your poison has failed.
CIRCE: What kind of man are you? Where do you come from?
    No-one, no-one at all, has ever been proof against
    My powers.
ODYSSEUS: My name is Odysseus.
            A gasp from Circe as his sword is drawn
    On your knees, witch, or my sword goes right through
    Your throat.
CIRCE: No! Let me live!
ODYSSEUS: Why, Circe, why should I? You have turned my men
    Into animals, here, in this very room . . .
CIRCE: Come Odysseus, sheathe your sword, and let us go
    To my room and pledge our friendship there in love
    And sleep.
ODYSSEUS: I see. Now you think, when you've lured me away,
    You'll steal my armour, make me weak and defenceless . . .
    Well, I will come with you, witch, but on one condition
    Only: you must swear a solemn and everlasting oath
    Not to harm me, not even to let the thought in your mind.

NARRATOR: Circe agreed, the oath was sworn, and they went to
    her room.
    Meanwhile, servants brought golden jugs of water,
    And a glittering silver bowl, ready for Odysseus to wash
    His hands. And when he came from Circe's room, they set
    Before him a polished table, spread with all the food
    A man could ever wish to eat.

    'Eat', said Circe – but Odysseus was sad, his thoughts
    Were elsewhere. Circe watched him, he never moved,

Didn't touch the food. She came up and spoke to him
Gently.

CIRCE: Why do you sit like that, Odysseus, as if you had lost
Your voice? Do you think there's another trick here?
You've nothing to fear. I've sworn my oath, and it binds me
For ever.

ODYSSEUS: Circe, how could a man who believes in right and justice
Bring himself to swallow food while his friends
Are prisoners? You tell me to eat. Well, if you mean it,
Set my men free.

NARRATOR: Circe picked up her wand and left the room. She went
To the pig pens, and drove out what looked like a herd
Of nine-year-old hogs. She made them stand in a row
In front of her, and went down the line rubbing each one
With a new drug. Where bristles had sprouted there was now
Human skin, and once more they were men – but younger
Men, far handsomer – taller, even, it seemed.
They caught sight of Odysseus, and one after another
Came over to shake his hand. There were tears in their eyes,
They could not speak for happiness. Circe joined them,
And said:

CIRCE: Go down to your ship, Odysseus, draw it up on the beach,
Store all your provisions and weapons in a cave,
And come back here with your brave sailors.

NARRATOR: Odysseus agreed. When he reached his ship his men
Crowded round with questions . . .

4th SAILOR What happened to the rest? . . .

5th SAILOR: Quick! Tell us! Are they all dead?

ODYSSEUS: Follow me back to Circe's house and you will see
Your friends there.

Cheers, babble of talk, cut short by . . .

EURYLOCHOS: Stop! . . . Stop, men!

Pause

4th SAILOR: Eurylochos!

EURYLOCHOS: I've been to that house. He's leading you into
danger.

ODYSSEUS: By all the gods in heaven, I've risked my life
For you, saved your friends, and now you make me out
A liar! But never again, Eurylochos, never again!

He draws his sword

Say goodbye to your head. . . .!

Hubbub

4th SAILOR: Hold him! . . .

5th SAILOR: Keep them apart . . .

4th SAILOR: He'll kill him!

ODYSSEUS: Let me go! I'll cut off his head!

4th SAILOR: Leave him alone, sir . . . Let him stay here and guard
   The ship. You show us the way to Circe's palace.
NARRATOR: So they all left the ship on the beach. Even
      Eurylochos
   Refused to be left behind – afraid what would happen
   If he defied Odysseus.

   Meanwhile, at her house, Circe had seated the men
   At a long table. They were well into dinner when Odysseus
   And the rest of the crew arrived. For a moment
   They stared at each other. Then they all let out
   A shout of joy, rushed into each other's arms,
   And filled the whole palace with noise.
   Circe came up and spoke to Odysseus:
CIRCE: Come, forget all you've suffered on your journey here.
   Eat, drink, pretend this is Ithaca, and you have not
   Yet left for the war. Be at peace, enjoy yourselves –
   Look how thin you are!
NARRATOR: She was right, and they did as she asked. The days
      passed
   In feasting and drinking, they had all they could ask for . . .
   The months came and went, the seasons changed, and a whole
   Year was spent in this way . . . Once more it was summer,
   And the days were long, and on one of those summer days
   The sailors came to Odysseus and called for a meeting.
1st SAILOR: Odysseus – remember, you have a home and a country
   Waiting. Are you ever to see them again – or is that
   Not to be?

NARRATOR: Odysseus knew what they meant. Late that evening,
   After dark, while his men slept in the night-shadowed palace,
   He went to Circe's room.
ODYSSEUS: Circe, my thoughts have taken me far away from here –
   To Ithaca, to my home. My sailors too. They give me
   No peace, they are pining to be gone. You do not see it,
   But they tell me what they feel.
CIRCE: Odysseus, you are no longer happy in my house,
   You must not stay here. But before you go, let me warn you
   Of what is to come on the long voyage ahead . . .
   First you will come to an island, with broad meadows,
   Where you will see women. These women have
   The most beautiful voices in the whole world.
   They are called Sirens, and they bewitch every man
   Who comes near them. You must know this:
   If you go close enough to hear their voices
   Your one desire will be to sit in the fields
   Where the Sirens sing, and listen, listen, listen . . .

But in those fields are piles of human bones, draped
With shreds of dried-up skin – all that is left of men
Who listened to the Sirens' songs. Avoid them. Sail
Out of earshot. Let none of you hear their voices.
After that your way will take you towards two islands.
One soars to the sky in a jagged peak, wreathed
In midnight clouds. Half way up is a cave, so high
Above the waves you could never reach it with an arrow
Shot from the deck of your ship.
In the hollows of that cave lives Scylla. Her voice
Is strange. She makes the squeaking sound of a new-born
Puppy – though she herself is a colossal monster.
She has twelve feet, all dangling and unformed.
She has six long necks, on each of which is a cruel head,
Crowded with three rows of teeth. All the teeth
Are stained black with dried blood. She sits half huddled
In her cave, with her six heads lolling out over
The chasm, and she fishes there, scanning the deep water
For dolphins, and sharks, and any other sea creature
She can find. Each of her six heads will snatch
A sailor from your crew. You must not try to resist
Or oppose her with your weapons.
The other island faces her across the gulf. It is a low rock
Called Charybdis. In the centre is a huge fig tree,
And beneath its spreading foliage lurks Charybdis herself,
Gulping down floods of the deep sea water, making a whirlpool.
Three times a day she swallows it,
Three times she disgorges it,
Her power is terrifying.
If you are near Charybdis when she gulps down the water
You are lost. Not even the great power who rules
The ocean could save you then. It's better to lose
Six of your men to Scylla, than have Charybdis take all.
Past Scylla and Charybdis you will come to a fertile land
Where many herds of cattle and flocks of fat sheep
Are grazing. They belong to the Sun, and are immortal.
They never have young, they never die. Don't touch them.
Remember – you are going home, think of nothing else.
If you do as I say, you will reach Ithaca, in spite
Of all your trials and sufferings. But if you slaughter
Those cattle then I can see disaster ahead for your ship
And your men. And even if you yourself escape,
It will only be after much danger and the death
Of all your friends.
NARRATOR: Circe had finished. Dawn was painting the sky with
    gold.

She went to walk in the forest, while Odysseus strode
Through the palace, rousing and cheering his men.

But even so there was sorrow in their leaving.
The youngest in the crew was a boy called Elpenor –
Not a very strong fighter, not a very clever brain.
The night before, looking for a cool place to sleep,
He had wandered off on his own and climbed the roof
Of Circe's house. And there, fuddled with wine,
He had fallen asleep. Now the noise of the men
Preparing to leave, and the sudden clatter of going,
Woke him up, and he forgot where he was. He scrambled
To his feet, rushed down from the roof – but not
By the ladder. Instead, he fell headlong, and broke
His neck. Sadly, his comrades buried him. They built
A mound and set up a stone to mark the place,
And planted Elpenor's oar above the tomb. Then
They all went down to the ship, and took their places
On the benches, and struck the sea to foam with their oars.
Circe of the flowing hair sent a following wind to fill
Their sails and see them on their way. She was a great
Goddess, and wise in these things. The men worked
On their armour and trimmed the ship, while the wind
And the helmsman carried them onward.

ODYSSEY

III Odysseus at Sea

CAST:

Narrator
Odysseus
The Sirens
Eurylochos
1st Sailor
2nd Sailor
3rd Sailor

NARRATOR: The ship bounded through the waves, and the wind
    held steady
  All the way from Circe's island. Closer they came
  To the land where the Sirens lived, closer, closer . . .
  The wind dropped . . . The air went still . . . they sat
  Becalmed.
  And Odysseus remembered the words of Circe:

ODYSSEUS: *To himself* An island with broad
  Meadows, and the voices of women singing.
  If we go close enough to hear,
  Our one desire will be to sit in the fields
  Where the Sirens sing, and listen, listen, listen . . .
  But in those fields are piles of human bones
  With shreds of dried-up skin – all that is left of men
  Who listened to the Sirens' songs. Sail on, sail
  Out of earshot. That's what she said.

NARRATOR: Odysseus sliced a disc of beeswax into pieces, began
  To knead it between his fingers.

ODYSSEUS: Listen, men, soon I shall ask you to tie me upright
  In the centre of the ship, tight as you can, and make sure
  I can't escape. If I beg you to set me free, even
  If I make it an order, you must only bind me tighter.

NARRATOR: While he talked the wax grew soft in the sun's heat.
  Odysseus went to each of the sailors in turn and stopped
  Their ears. Then they tied him hand and foot to the mast
  With lengths of rigging, and left him standing there.
  Smoothly and strongly they began to row – the sea
  Turned white beneath their oars . . . They were speeding
  Along, just as far from land as a man's voice would carry,
  When the Sirens noticed the ship passing, and began to sing.
  Their voices pierced deep into Odysseus' soul.

SIRENS: Turn your ship,
  Odysseus, master of men's minds, this way, this way.
  Stay with us, listen to the songs we sing. There is all joy
  In them, and a new world to hear of. We know the secrets
  Of the earth and sea – do you want to hear them. . . .?

ODYSSEUS: Yes, I want to, with all my heart I want to!

SIRENS: Then beach your ship and listen.

ODYSSEUS: Beach the ship, men! I want to hear!

SIRENS: Listen, Odysseus, listen to us . . .

ODYSSEUS: I want to! . . . Set me free, men, let me hear them . . .

NARRATOR: Odysseus signalled with frowns and looks to his men
  To free him. But the men leaned on their oars, and rowed,
  While two of them jumped to their feet and wound
  Still more rope round Odysseus, pulling it tighter
  Than ever . . . And so they sailed on past the island,

And at last he could hear the sound of the Sirens' voices
No more. Then the men took the wax out of their ears
And untied Odysseus.

No sooner was the island over the horizon than they saw
A cloud of vapour and a monster wave ahead, and heard
The sound of waves drumming on rocks. They were terrified.
The oars slipped from their hands and splashed down
Into the water. Without the oarstrokes to drive her
Forwards the ship began to lose way. Odysseus went down
The line of his men, urging them on, calming them,
Giving them courage.

ODYSSEUS: Friends, we are used to danger – and this is no worse
Than when Cyclops captured and bottled us up in his cave.
We escaped that time because I thought for us all,
I used my wits, and took command. Think of that now –
And row – row hard! And you, helmsman, remember this:
Keep the ship on a course straight for that high rock –
Steer as far as you can from that big wave you see.
If you're careless, and allow the ship to drift that way,
You'll sink us all.

NARRATOR: The warning of Circe was in his mind:

ODYSSEUS: *To himself* Two islands,
On one side, Scylla, high up the jagged rock,
A monster with six long necks, six cruel heads,
Scanning the deep water.
And close on the other side, the whirlpool Charybdis,
And our way lies between.

NARRATOR: But forgetting Circe's good advice
Not to resist, or oppose her with his weapons,
Odysseus put on his coat of mail,
Balanced two long spears in his hands, and went up
To the stern. It was there he expected Scylla to strike.
With his weapons poised he searched the mists draped
Round the high crag, but she was nowhere to be seen.
All he did was strain his eyes . . . On they sailed . . .
Now they were in the narrow gorge with Scylla on one side
And Charybdis on the other. They quivered with fear
To see Charybdis suck down the salty sea-water
With a gurgling roar – then vomit it up again,
Making the sea growl and seethe like a cauldron
Set on a hot fire. High in the air spray dashed
Against both rocks, while far below them the sea bed
Was laid bare, dyed black with silt stirred up
From the depths. Gripped with fright the sailors
Went pale. They stared at Charybdis as if they saw

Death itself . . . And that was the moment Scylla chose
To strike!

    Screams – shouts

Odysseus whirled round to see six pairs of feet
And hands waving in the air above him. They belonged
To six of his bravest fighters and staunchest sailors,
And each of Scylla's six heads had seized a man.
The poor victims looked like fish, hooked at the end
Of a long rod by a fisherman, who lifts them gasping
And wriggling out of the water and tosses them on to land.
Just so were the sailors hoisted out of the ship by Scylla
All the way up to her cave, where she devoured them.
They screamed, over and over they screamed, and stretched
Their hands out in stark terror . . . Of all the things
Odysseus had seen in his long travels that was the one
That hurt him hardest and caused him to suffer the most.

But he was helpless. Already that terrible cliff
Was behind them, they were past Scylla and Charybdis,
And they were sailing towards an island kept holy
And pure for an eternal power. Here were grazing
The broad-faced cattle and swarming fat flocks
Of mighty Apollo, the Sun-God himself. From far out at sea
Odysseus could hear the cattle lowing in the fields,
And the bleating of the sheep. And then the warning
Of Circe came back to him . . .

ODYSSEUS: Friends, I want you to row on past this island . . .
Helmsman, bear out to sea!

EURYLOCHOS: Odysseus! Have you no feelings left? Do you **never**
Get tired?

ODYSSEUS: I'm just as exhausted as anyone here, Eurylochos,
    but Circe
Told me this island belongs to the God of the Sun, and she said
To avoid it. She said that terrible misfortune could befall us
Here. So sail on.

EURYLOCHOS: And not even eat? Not even set foot on land? Sail
on, you say,
Without sleep – who knows where? Over a sea shrouded in mist?

1st SAILOR: And the night winds, sir – those winds are bad,
    treacherous . . .

2nd SAILOR: They're ship-wreck winds . . .

3rd SAILOR: Yes, and there's no moon tonight.

1st SAILOR: Where do we go if a storm blows up?

ODYSSEUS: We can't land here. It's too dangerous.

EURYLOCHOS: We'll stay with the ship, not move a step inland,
And at first light we'll set sail again.

2nd SAILOR: He's right, Eurylochos is right . . .

1st SAILOR: We're not iron men, like our captain . . .

3rd SAILOR: Heave to . . .

2nd SAILOR: Drop anchor here . . .

1st SAILOR: I say we land!

ODYSSEUS: I'm captain, and I say we sail on.

EURYLOCHOS: You may be captain, but there are more of us.

ODYSSEUS: Do you stand by him – or by me?

SAILORS: Eurylochos . . . Eurylochos is right . . .

ODYSSEUS: I see.

> *Brief pause*

Well, since I can't force you, I have no choice.
We land here. But first I want you to swear
A solemn oath to me . . . Will you do it?

1st SAILOR: Fair enough . . .

3rd SAILOR: We'll swear.

ODYSSEUS: On my sword, then . . . We swear – come on, repeat it.
We swear . . .

SAILORS: We swear . . .

ODYSSEUS: To regard as sacred . . .

SAILORS: To regard as sacred . . .

ODYSSEUS: All the animals . . .

SAILORS: All the animals . . .

ODYSSEUS: Living on this island.

SAILORS: Living on this island.

ODYSSEUS: Good. Mind you keep your word.

NARRATOR: They anchored their ship in a sheltered bay,
   near a spring
Of crystal water. They jumped ashore, and prepared some food.
Sadly, they ate their meal, thinking of the friends
They had lost in the jaws of Scylla. Still grieving,
They lay down to sleep, and for a while forgot their sorrow.
It was the third watch of the night, and the stars had set,
When Zeus sent down a blustering wind with a tremendous clap
Of thunder, and enveloped land and water alike with clouds.
Night charged down from the heavens. When dawn came
The sailors dragged their ship into a deep wide cave,
And docked her there to wait for favouring weather.
But that wind came from the south, and it blew without cease
For a whole month, and if it changed at all it was only
To let the east wind blow. So long as their store of food
And wine lasted the sailors clung on to life, and stayed
In the cave. But the day came when all the stores
In their ship were gone, and they were forced to go out
Hunting fish, birds, anything they could find in the crooked
Inlets. Hunger clawed at their stomachs.

Odysseus went away inland to pray and meditate alone . . .
Perhaps some idea would come, some inspiration, some way
Of escape. He found a place sheltered from the wind,
And sat there summoning help from the powers of spirit
And soul. His eyelids drooped, a sweet sensation poured
Through him. He was asleep.
Meanwhile, his men were discussing their plight.

EURYLOCHOS: Listen, friends, death is nasty enough, however
   it comes,
But death by starvation is the most horrible end of all
To a life. I say we should show our respect for the god Appollo,
Build him an altar to prove it, and then kill some
Of his cattle. He can have the best as a gift from us.
And if he's angry with us for wanting to stay alive
And decides to sink our ship – well, I'd rather die
A quick death from a mouthful of sea than wither away
To nothing on this desolate island here.
      Murmur of agreement
Good. Then see that young bullock over there? Catch him!
This way . . .
      Lowing of cattle
Drive him this way!

1st SAILOR: Tame, isn't he?

EURYLOCHOS: And fat.

2nd SAILOR: Seems to think we're his friends.

3rd SAILOR: We are. We love him.

1st SAILOR: They're not used to strangers. They've never been
   hunted.

2nd SAILOR: Forgive us, Apollo, God of the Sun, we're hungry
   men.

1st SAILOR: Perhaps we should pray first.

3rd SAILOR: No. Eat now. Pray later.

NARRATOR: They surrounded the cattle, picked out the best,
Slaughtered them, skinned them, and carved them up
Into joints. They skewered the meat, lit a fire, and began
To roast the beef . . .
At this moment the sleep that had made him forget the world
Slid away from Odysseus. He began to walk back to the beach,
But as he came near the place where his ship lay
The smell of freshly cooked meat was blown towards him
On the breeze. He groaned, muttered a prayer,
And started to run . . .

ODYSSEUS: Stop! You fools! . . . Stop – you brainless
   Gluttonous blasphemous pigs! . . . What have you done?

3rd SAILOR: Had a beautiful dinner.

ODYSSEUS: Half-wit! Didn't you swear an oath? Didn't you swear

To keep your hands off those cattle?

EURYLOCHOS: We were hungry. Do you want us to starve?

ODYSSEUS: You'll wish you had when Apollo takes his revenge!

1st SAILOR: What does it matter now? The cattle are dead,
And nothing's happened.

3rd SAILOR: Yes it has. My belt's burst.

ODYSSEUS: Butchers! Murderers!

Lowing of cattle

2nd SAILOR: What was that?

EURYLOCHOS: Cattle.

1st SAILOR: I don't see any cattle.

3rd SAILOR: We killed them all.

EURYLOCHOS: Must be one somewhere. Perhaps one got away ...

2nd SAILOR: It's the meat!

EURYLOCHOS: What?

2nd SAILOR: The meat – making that noise!

EURYLOCHOS: It can't be. We carved it up.

2nd SAILOR: It is. It's still alive. Listen ...

Lowing

The raw meat's alive!

3rd SAILOR: So's this on the fire. It's coming from here, too ...

Lowing as from a whole herd

1st SAILOR: Look, something's moving!

EURYLOCHOS: Where?

1st SAILOR: Over there.

EURYLOCHOS: Don't be a fool, that's a skinned hide.

1st SAILOR: I saw it move. It moved along the ground.

EURYLOCHOS: You're mad. We killed it. It's an empty hide, that's
all.

1st SAILOR: Look, it's crawling ...

3rd SAILOR: It's creeping this way ...

Lowing, shouts from the men

ODYSSEUS: Quickly, launch the ship – fast as you can.
These are signs from heaven ...

EURYLOCHOS: Come on, men, the place is haunted. I knew
We should never have landed here ...

Running on beach, ship launched into sea

ODYSSEUS: Man the oars ... Into your places! I'll take the helm.
Hurry! Hurry!

In the background, lowing and monstrous sounds

Now – one – out! Two – out! Faster, faster ...!

The lowing fades and oar and sea sounds rise

NARRATOR: They left that island far behind them. It vanished
Over the horizon, and soon there was nothing in all
The world but sea and sky. Suddenly a blue-black cloud
Formed right above the ship. Zeus had sent it. The sea

Beneath turned the colour of ink. For a short way the ship
Held on her course, till a sudden clap of thunder cracked
The air, a west wind pounced, howling, and the force
Of the gale snapped the ropes holding the mast – which toppled
Backwards, leaving rigging tangled all over the deck.
The falling mast struck the helmsman on the head,
Splintered his skull, and spilled his brains out.
Like a man diving, he plummeted from the steering platform,
Dead as his bones hit the waves. More thunder and then
A bolt of lightning blazed down on the ship. She swirled
Completely round beneath the blow, tilted, and filled
With water. The men were tumbled from the deck and tossed
In the waves like a flock of birds in a storm.
God had said no to their hopes of home.
Odysseus was darting through the ship when a wave
Loosened the sides from the keel, and washed the keel
Away on its own. The mast broke off, and Odysseus sank
Under the foaming waves. For some time, weighed down
By his clothing, he could not swim, but at last
He surfaced and spat the bitter sea water out of his mouth
As it streamed down his head. He was almost out of strength
When he saw the mast . . . It was floating past him.
He stripped off the clothes that weighed him down,
And struggled towards it. Half dead, he reached out,
Hung on, then dragged himself up until he was astride
The mast like a horseman astride his mount. And there
He stayed, tossed this way, that way, by the waves,
The way flowers are swept over the ground in clusters
By an autumn north wind. First the south gave him
To the north to play with; then the east passed him over
To the west to chase.
For two nights and two days in the lathered sea he drifted,
And often death stooped down and clouded his spirit.
But when dawn came on the third day the wind dropped,
And the storm abated. Raised on the crest of a wave
Odysseus peered round, and there, just visible, he saw it –
Land! To Odysseus that sight of land was life and hope,
Like the sight of their father to children, when he comes out
Safe from a long sickness which has brought him close
To death. Odysseus began to swim, striking out for the feel
Of land beneath his feet. When he was shouting distance
Away from the shore he heard the sound of waves clashing
On rocks. The sea was shattered into white foam
As it broke with an explosion of surf against a jutting
Headland, and spray rose in a veil over everything.
There was no anchorage for ships, no safe harbour,

Only cliffs, rocks, headlands, and reefs. Then Odysseus
Was afraid; the strength drained from his limbs, his heart
Sank.

ODYSSEUS: Did Zeus save me for this? To struggle and conquer the ocean,
To reach land, look at it once, and after all that –
To be trapped in the sea, never allowed to escape!

NARRATOR: While these thoughts whirled in his brain, a great wave
Swelled up and carried him forwards to a jagged rock.
The skin would have all been ripped from his flesh
And his bones smashed if he had not hung on grimly to the rock
With both hands, until the wave died down. Then he slipped
Back, and the rush of receding water sucked him out to sea.
Have you seen an octopus dragged from his hiding place?
Dozens of pebbles cling to his tentacles. In just the same way
Strips of skin from Odysseus' hands were left hanging
On the rocks as the great wave engulfed him.
When he surfaced again, the water was surging inland again.
Odysseus began to swim parallel to the shore, looking
For any sloping beaches or sandy places or harbours.
He paddled along till he came opposite the mouth
Of a river. This seemed the most likely place. It was bare
Of rocks, and sheltered from the wind. But then he noticed
The river's powerful current. He muttered a heartfelt prayer.

ODYSSEUS: Spirit of this river, whoever you are, hear my prayer.
I have been hunted by storms and angry seas, I am lost
And near death. Pity me, lord, I am at your mercy.

NARRATOR: Whatever spirit it was that ruled that river heard Odysseus.
He stopped the flow of his stream, the current slowed,
The river was still, and allowed Odysseus safely
Into his estuary. In the shallow water his legs folded up
Beneath him, his arms went limp – the sea had broken
His spirit. All his flesh was swollen, and the sea water
Had bloated his mouth and nostrils. Struggling for breath,
Unable to speak, he floated there, more dead than alive.
A cruel exhaustion swept through him. At last he could breathe
Once more, he regained his strength, and tottered
Out of the water to crumple full length in a bed of reeds.
He kissed the earth – the earth, giver of life.
Then he began to think.

ODYSSEUS: If I spend the night next to this river, the frost and damp
Will finish me off. I'm nearly dead as it is, and when dawn
Comes, a freezing wind will blow off the water. If I climb
The banks and lie down in the bushes of that thick wood

The shivering and tiredness will leave me, and I can sleep –
Yes, but what if there are wild animals hunting for food,
And what if the food they find is me . . .?

NARRATOR: At last he fixed on a plan. He went into the wood
and found
A clearing near the river, where two bushes grew
Out of the same spot of earth. He pulled them together
To make a tent of leaves. Beneath their interlacing branches
He was safe from the wind's damp breath, and the burning
Of the sun's rays and the showers of rain. For a bed
Odysseus made a thick mattress out of the leaves that were lying
All around in heaps. They were piled so high they could keep
Three men warm in midwinter, in the coldest season.
Grateful for rest, Odysseus lay down in the middle,
And heaped more leaves on top of himself, as one who conceals
A live coal in earth to keep the seed of fire alive.
Then Athene, his guardian spirit, poured sleep in his eyes
To ease him as fast as she could from the fatigue
That racked his body. His eyelids drooped. He was asleep.

ODYSSEY
IV Nausicaa

CAST:

Narrator
Odysseus
Athene, goddess of wisdom
Nausicaa, the princess
Alcinoös, king of Phaeacia
Old Man
Noble
Eumaios, the swineherd
Men
Girls

NARRATOR: Odysseus slept in his tent of leaves. His long
And terrible struggle with the sea had stolen all
His strength.
In a nearby city lived a people called Phaeacians.
Their king had a daughter, Nausicaa, and while she slept
That night Nausicaa had a dream. In her dream the goddess
Athene, friend of Odysseus, appeared, and spoke to her.
Supernatural sound
ATHENE: Nausicaa, how careless you are. Your beautiful clothes
Lie forgotten, tossed aside in a corner. Tomorrow,
As soon as the sun rises, you should go and wash them.
You'll soon be a bride, and at your wedding all you wear
Must be purest white.
Supernatural sound
NARRATOR: The figure vanished. Athene glided back to Olympos,
Where immortal spirits live. The sun's first rays
Woke Nausicaa, but her strange dream lingered, and she went
To look for her father. She met him going out
With his nobles and chieftains to a council of state.

NAUSICAA: Father . . . Father . . . Wait . . .!
Father, I want to take all my dresses down to the river
Today, and wash them. I'm going to take your clothes as well
So you can sit in your council chamber in freshly laundered
Robes – and then my brothers are always asking
For clean clothes to go out dancing, so I'll take theirs too,
All five of them. For all that clothing I need a horse
And cart.
ALCINOÖS: You can have whatever you want, my child.
Servants – go and harness a pair of horses.
NARRATOR: Nausicaa collected the dirty clothes from the palace.
Her mother prepared a delicious meal, and put it
In a hamper. The princess climbed into the cart,
Her servants sat behind, she picked up the whip,
Cracked it over the horses' heads, rattled the reins,
And with a clatter of hooves and wheels they were off . . .

Nausicaa and her servants reached the stream, but Odysseus
Heard nothing. He slept on while the girls went about
Their work.
The river was sparkling clear, with rock-pools for washing,
And a flood of bright water gushed into them
And out again, making worn and dirty clothes like new.
They unharnessed the horses from the cart, and shooed them
Away to graze in the deep sweet grass at the river's edge.
Then they took out the bundles of clothing, and soaked them
In a dark pool, and trod out the dirt in the rock-basins,

Racing to see who could do it quickest.
When they had washed the dirt out of all the clothes,
They spread them in a line on the sea shore, where the waves
Had left the shingle smooth and scrubbed, and sat down
To eat on the banks of the stream while they waited
For the clothes to dry in the sunshine.
When their meal was over Nausicaa and her servants
Took off their veils to play a game. Nausicaa began a song
And they tossed a ball from hand to hand in time
To the words. White arms flashed, and round and round
Went the ball until the princess threw too hard,
Missed her servant, the ball fell in the deepest part
Of the river, and swirled downstream. They shrieked –
And Odysseus woke up.

ODYSSEUS: Where am I? . . . Who are these people? . . . Careful
now,
May be danger here . . .
   Rustle of leaves
Just girls – no one else . . . I'll speak to them . . . Wait!
I can't go out naked like this. I need some cover –
A branch . . . This'll do.
   He breaks a branch
Not the most elegant dress I've ever worn, but at least
I'm fit for company . . . Now . . .
   Walking through leaves

NARRATOR: Odysseus walked out of the forest. Streaked with brine
And bruised by the sea, looking fierce as a mountain lion,
He presented a grim sight to the girls.
   They scream
They ran. They ran in all directions. Only Nausicaa,
The princess, was not afraid. She stood her ground,
Faced him, straight and proud, and her knees never trembled.
Odysseus spoke to her with all the grace and courtesy
At his command.

ODYSSEUS: Your Highness, before your beauty and your stately
bearing
I am lost for words. Should I call you 'princess',
Or am I perhaps addressing the goddess Artemis herself?
Whichever you are, my lady, have mercy on me. I am
A poor ship-wrecked sailor, cast up on your shore.
Last night I escaped the perils of the sea. But am I
Any safer here? Give me your word that I am.

NAUSICAA: Stranger, I think you are honest. You look honest –
And kind . . . You are a guest in my country now.
Whatever you need you shall have, and what you need most
At this moment, I see, is clothes . . .

Servants, look – this man is perfectly harmless. Don't
Run away. Bring him some clothes, let him wash in the river.
He's our guest now . . .

NARRATOR: They showed Odysseus the way to a sheltered pool.
He scooped up water, washed off the brine that caked
His back and broad shoulders, and scraped away the salt
Encrusted in his hair from the chilling waves.
When he was clean he put on the clothes they had given him,
And stood up straight again. Now he was changed – taller,
Broader than before, his hair thick and glossy
Like dark hyacinth. Sometimes a goldsmith,
Skilled in his craft, will gild a piece of silverware
And make it glow with the splendour of the sun.
Odysseus, strong and tall, glowed like that, and Nausicaa
Marvelled at the change in him. She wished she could meet
A man like that in her own country, who would ask her
To marry him. She came over, and spoke to Odysseus.
NAUSICAA: Hurry, stranger, we're going back to the city now.
This is my plan: as long as we are riding through
The countryside you can sit with us on the cart.
But when we reach the city walls we must be careful
Of the crowds. People are cruel and envious.
They'll jeer at us: 'Who's the tall handsome stranger
With Nausicaa? Where did she find him? Has she got herself
A husband? Pity she couldn't find a man here in Phaeacia.'
Words like that can stab to the heart. So when we are still
Outside the city walls, you stay behind, give us time
To reach the palace, and then, when you think
We're safely home, you follow us into the city
And ask where King Alcinoös lives. He is my father
And everyone knows his palace.
NARRATOR: And so they left the river and rolled through the
fields
In the evening light . . .

Later that night Odysseus walked through the crowded streets
Till he found the palace of the king. At the entrance
He paused. He stood in the doorway, not daring to cross
The gorgeous threshold, all gold and silver, glittering
Like the rays of the sun and moon together. Inside,
King Alcinoös was sitting at dinner with his queen
And court. Odysseus collected his thoughts, opened the door,
Walked in, past guards, nobles, and courtiers, and went
Straight to the feet of the queen herself. Everyone
Was amazed when they saw this man striding through
Their midst. The room went silent, as Odysseus knelt.

ODYSSEUS: Queen, I am here to ask you and all your guests for
　　help.
　　My request is simple. Send me home to my own country.
　　　　Pause – murmurs
OLD MAN: Your Majesty, here is a stranger, kneeling at the feet
　　Of the queen, asking for help, and we just leave him
　　There. It's shameful! No one dares to speak
　　Because we are all waiting for you.
　　But I am the oldest here, I have counselled you
　　In peace and war, and I am not afraid. I say
　　You should give this man a chair, and have one
　　Of your servants bring him something to eat.
ALCINOÖS: You are right . . . Stranger, you may stand up.
　　Give me your hand.
　　Good . . . Laodamas, my son, give our friend
　　Your place . . . Master of Ceremonies, bring wine,
　　And let us all drink the stranger's health . . . I want
　　This understood by everyone here – this man is our guest.
　　While he is in our country he is to be given
　　All the protection and courtesy he requires. Perhaps
　　He is a god from heaven. Gods come in disguise
　　And walk among men sometimes.
ODYSSEUS: No, my lord, I am nothing like a god. I am a man,
　　No more. My one distinction is – I have seen
　　More suffering and pain than any man alive.
　　And the one thing I ask before I die is to see
　　My house, my family, and my own land again.
NOBLE: I say he deserves our help.
OTHERS: Agreed, agreed . . .
ALCINOÖS: You think we should do what the stranger asks?
ALL: Yes, yes, certainly, yes . . .
ALCINOÖS: Well, sir, you shall have your wish. My fastest ship
　　Will be ready tomorrow to take you wherever you want to go.
ODYSSEUS: Thank you, Alcinoös, may heaven bless your house
　　And your children for ever more.
ALCINOÖS: And now tell us, stranger, who are you, where do you
　　Come from, and who gave you those clothes you're wearing?
　　They seem familiar, like some clothes I once had myself.
ODYSSEUS: Your Majesty, I was ship-wrecked several days ago.
　　Since then I have been adrift on the sea, and last night
　　I managed to swim ashore on your land. I fell asleep,
　　And half way through today the sun's heat woke me.
　　I saw some women, servants I thought, washing clothes
　　At the river, and playing. One of them was a noble
　　And beautiful girl, like a goddess . . .
ALCINOÖS: Nausicaa!

ODYSSEUS: You know her?

ALCINOÖS: It was my daughter you saw.

ODYSSEUS: A worthy daughter of a great king. Her spirit is as fine
As her looks. She was not afraid of me. She gave me food,
And she gave me these clothes . . .

ALCINOÖS: Now I'm angry with her. She did wrong!

ODYSSEUS: Why? Because she was kind to me?

ALCINOÖS: Because she was not kind enough. She should have brought you
Home herself, not left you to find your way alone.

ODYSSEUS: No, don't blame her for that. I can imagine your thoughts
If we had arrived together. You would have been suspicious –
Angry . . .

ALCINOÖS: No, stranger, no, I don't lose my temper unless I have good
Reason. I can see what kind of man you are, and by Zeus
In heaven, I wish you could stay here with us, and marry
My daughter, and be a new son to me. I'd give you a house,
And land . . .

ODYSSEUS: I have a wife, your majesty, and she waits for me now.

ALCINOÖS: Well, no one here will keep you from her. I shall see to
Your ship, and tomorrow you will start your journey home.
Meanwhile, you are tired, so sleep.

ODYSSEUS: I pray to heaven your fame never dies, Alcinoös,
And may all you wish for in this life come true.

NARRATOR: And so Odysseus was made welcome, and he slept sound
That night in a soft bed in the King's palace.
The next morning they all went down to the harbour –
The king, the queen, the courtiers, the people of the city –
To watch Odysseus board the ship Alcinoös had given him.
He went and sat in the stern, where they had spread
Carpets and sheets for him to rest on. A box of gifts
Was lifted on board, presents from Alcinoös to Odysseus,
The crew climbed into their places, and they cast off.
Bent over their oars, they sent the ship leaping
Across the sea, and left the waves flashing and shouting
In their wake. Not even the hawk, fastest bird that flies,
Could keep up with a ship sailed by those men from Phaeacia.
They slit the sea open – their cargo, a man who had seen
A whole world of suffering, lifetimes of sorrow and wisdom,
Who had survived wars, the loss of friends, and the sea's
Rage. This man now, as night fell, lay motionless
In sleep, and all his ordeals were forgotten.
The star that comes to herald dawn was shining clear

And bright above the mast when the great vessel glided
Towards the island of Ithaca. There was a lonely beach,
Guarded by cliffs that locked out the wind, where ships
Could ride without anchor. Here they touched land
And leapt ashore. First they lifted out Odysseus,
Still fast asleep, and laid him on the sand, bed and all.
Then they took out the gifts the generous Phaeacians
Had given him and piled them under a nearby tree.
There they left him, and stole away to start the long
Voyage home. A mist came in from the sea, and at dawn
Odysseus woke.

ODYSSEUS: *Yawns* What is this place? . . .
Phaeacian fools! . . . Said they'd take me to Ithaca . . .
But did they do it? No they did not! They've left me
Stranded on some patch of desert.
> *Supernatural sound*

ATHENE: Good morning.

ODYSSEUS: Who are you? Where did you come from?

ATHENE: Out of the mist.

ODYSSEUS: Do you live here?

ATHENE: I have a home here, yes.

ODYSSEUS: What country is this?

ATHENE: You must have travelled far, stranger. Everyone knows
This place.

ODYSSEUS: I don't. Is it an island . . . part of the mainland . . .?

ATHENE: This is an island, stranger, a famous island. Its name
Is Ithaca.

ODYSSEUS: *passionately* Heaven be praised!

ATHENE: Why?

ODYSSEUS: *recovering his caution* What do you mean?

ATHENE: Why praise heaven? Does Ithaca mean so much to you?

ODYSSEUS: *casually* I've heard of Ithaca, of course, who has not?
Even in Crete, far across the sea – Crete is where
I come from – well, even in Crete we have heard of Ithaca.
I arrived last night, on business, with all my possessions. . .
Why are you laughing?

ATHENE: Oh Odysseus, Odysseus, will you ever be plain
And straightforward?

ODYSSEUS: What?

ATHENE: No, don't back away.

ODYSSEUS: I don't trust you . . .

ATHENE: You've come home, Odysseus, no need to pretend any
more,
No need to make mysteries . . .

ODYSSEUS: Tell me your name!
> *He draws his sword*

I order you to . . .
Supernatural sound
Pallas Athene! Goddess!

ATHENE: Now you know me.

ODYSSEUS: You are too clever for me, Athene. You say I make
Mysteries, but I cannot mystify you.

ATHENE: We are two of a kind, Odysseus. You, master of men
In guile and tactics; I, daughter of Zeus, first
Of the gods in wisdom and strategy.

ODYSSEUS: And am I really back in Ithaca?

ATHENE: Look.
Supernatural sound
Rise, mist, and let Odysseus see his lands, his fields,
His forests and hills . . .
Supernatural sound
Island of Ithaca – your king is home!

ODYSSEUS: Home! My country, my own dear land!

ATHENE: Hurry, Odysseus, we have work to do. First we'll hide
Your treasure in a cave close by to make sure it's safe.
And then we must lay our plans . . . This way . . .
Fade to cave interior
Cover it with sand. So. No-one will find it here . . .
Now listen, Odysseus. For three years all the nobles
And chieftains on this island have been coming
To visit your wife. They want her to take a new husband,
Who will rule as king in your place.

ODYSSEUS: What does she say?

ATHENE: She gives them nothing but promises. But they are
determined
To make her marry one of them. They camp at your house,
Eat your food, drink your wine, ruin your property,
And refuse to leave till she chooses.

ODYSSEUS: Where is my son, Telemachos?

ATHENE: Telemachos has gone in search of you; he is travelling
All over Greece, asking everyone he meets for news
Of your fate . . .

ODYSSEUS: Have I any friends, anyone at all loyal to me?

ATHENE: Yes, one or two, you shall know them.

ODYSSEUS: How? Help me, Athene. I'll kill the chieftains, kill
Every last one of them!

ATHENE: You will have your revenge, Odysseus, but it must
be done
Cleverly. First, we must make sure no one knows
You're here. We'll give you a disguise . . . What shall it be?
Yes . . . I think we'll make you a tramp, a very old
And dirty tramp.

ODYSSEUS: But Athene, I wouldn't know how to . . .
ATHENE: Skin – wrinkle!

Thick hair – disappear!

Clear eyes – grow milky and dim!

Limbs – bend and weaken!

Clothes – become rags!

You make a very convincing tramp, Odysseus. Not even
Your own wife and son would know you now.
ODYSSEUS: What do I do? I've never gone begging in my life!
ATHENE: First, go to your swineherd, Eumaios. He is loyal.
Wait at his hut, and I will go and bring your son home.
Don't worry, Odysseus, your rivals
And enemies have only a few more days to live.
We shall meet again soon . . .
ODYSSEUS: When? . . . Where?
               Supernatural sound
Don't leave me, Athene!
ATHENE: *going* Soon . . . Soon . . .
NARRATOR: Athene vanished.
And Odysseus, disguised as a tramp, his head bald, his clothing
All rags, climbed the steep path to the hut where his old
Servant and swineherd, Eumaios, lived.
Suddenly the watchdogs, who would bark at the slightest sound,
Bounded towards him snarling.
Odysseus dropped his stick, and stood there, calm,
Prepared. But even so, there, on his own property,
He would have been torn to pieces, if Eumaios
Had not rushed through the door of his hut and scattered
The dogs with shouts and a hail of stones. Then he spoke
To King Odysseus:
EUMAIOS: Well, old tramp, my dogs nearly shortened your life
    for you –
And then I'd have had your death on my conscience . . .
And I've troubles enough, god knows, I've enough
To worry me. I sit here thinking of my master in grief
And sorrow. He was a fine brave man, but now I fatten
His herds of pigs for others to eat while he, I'm sure,
Is lost, starving, a stranger in a far country . . . if he still
Lives, that is. But come inside, old fellow, fill yourself
With as much food and wine as you want, and tell me
Where you've come from and what your troubles are.
               They go into the hut, the door closes
Sit down, stranger . . . Here, take this fleece,

It's wild goat, good and thick and warm – I use it
For a quilt myself.

ODYSSEUS: Whatever your prayers may be, my friend, I hope Zeus
And all the gods in heaven answer them. You are a kind host.

EUMAIOS: No, stranger, I turn nobody away from my door. The
poor
And wretched – and there are worse than you – they're all
Sent by God. I did what I have to do.

ODYSSEUS: Who is your master?

EUMAIOS: Odysseus, a great king.

ODYSSEUS: Is he at his palace now, or away at war?

EUMAIOS: Who knows where he is? Twenty years he's been away.
Some say he's alive – who knows?

NARRATOR: Eumaios got up and went out to the pig-sties, where
the animals
Were kept, chose two suckling pigs, and slaughtered them.
He singed off the bristles, chopped up the meat, and put it
On spits to roast at the fire. When they were brown
He brought them, sizzling, to Odysseus, sat down himself
Opposite, and said encouragingly:

EUMAIOS: Eat, stranger. It's the food of slaves – piglet. The suitors
Get all the fattened hogs. They have no respect or pity
In their hearts, those suitors.

ODYSSEUS: Suitors?

EUMAIOS: The island chieftains here. They've heard somewhere
God knows where, that my poor master is dead. And now
They want his wife Penelope. But they can't win her honestly.
She is a brave woman, a clever woman, she will not be lured
Away. She loves her husband, and means to stay true
To him. The suitors, though, they refuse to go back to their
Own homes. Instead,
They calmly sit there, on his land, in his palace,
Eating up his food! No one is strong enough to throw them
Out. Wine flows, no one stops them, no one cares.
Waste, waste! . . .

ODYSSEUS: Perhaps your master is alive after all.

EUMAIOS: No, stranger, no, we'll never hear of him again.
We've had plenty of people come with stories of how
They've seen him alive – hoping to please his wife,
But they were all lies, all just wanted money, you see.

ODYSSEUS: You trust nobody, then?

EUMAIOS: Who can you trust?

ODYSSEUS: What if I told you, on oath, that Odysseus is coming?

EUMAIOS: I wouldn't believe you. I'd know you were trying
To get something out of me. No, Odysseus will never
Come home . . . Drink up now, don't remind me

Of all that. I'd rather not think of him. It hurts me
Too much when I think of my good kind master . . .
NARRATOR: Night had come on as they talked. It was dark and
   moonless,
The weather was bad, and the sky poured rain all night
With a soaking wind from the west. Eumaios threw
A thick cloak round his shoulders to cheat the wind,
Picked up a spear, and went outside to guard the pigs
From stray dogs and robbers. All night long he sat
Under a rock out of the whistling wind, thinking of his master.
And he was weeping, because he thought Odysseus was dead.

ODYSSEY

V Odysseus in Disguise

CAST:

Narrator
Odysseus
Penelope, his wife
Telemachos, his son
Eurycleia, his old nurse
Eumaios, the swineherd
Athene, goddess of wisdom
Antinoös, a suitor
Iros, a beggar
1st suitor
2nd suitor
Sailor

NARRATOR: While Odysseus rested and gathered strength in
     the hut
Of his swineherd, Eumaios, his son Telemachos was hurrying
Home to Ithaca, summoned by a dream in which the goddess
Athene had warned him of danger if he stayed too long away
From his country. As he sailed towards Ithaca her words
Were in his head, as if borne on the wind . . .

ATHENE: *In a whisper* Telemachos, you are far from home, go back,
     Go back to Ithaca, and see what is happening there.
The suitors eat your food, steal your property,
And they give your mother no peace. They will force her
To marry one of them. Back to Ithaca, Telemachos.
When you touch land, send your men to the city,
But don't you go with them. Go to your servant, Eumaios,
To Eumaios . . .
          A knock on the door

EUMAIOS: Who's there?
          Opening the door
Master!

TELEMACHOS: Good morning, Eumaios.

EUMAIOS: It's like seeing my own son again . . . Are you all right,
     Master, come to no harm, have you?

TELEMACHOS: No, I'm safe and well . . .

EUMAIOS: Because I thought I'd never see you again, after you
     went off.
Come inside, come inside, leave your sword
At the door . . .
          They go inside
We have a guest, you see . . .

TELEMACHOS: Sit down, stranger, I'll find a chair somewhere,
     plenty
Of room.

EUMAIOS: Drink some of this, Telemachos . . . Are you
Hungry?

TELEMACHOS: I'll eat whatever you have, I'm starving.

EUMAIOS: Here – left over from last night's dinner.

TELEMACHOS: Thank you. *He eats.* Who's the stranger? Where
     does he come from?

EUMAIOS: Says he's from Crete, says he's been all over the world.
He came asking for shelter, so I took him in.

TELEMACHOS: Eumaios, you make me ashamed. You can have
     guests, but I
Can't. How could I bring a guest to my house,
With those suitors lording it everywhere?
          To Odysseus
Stranger, I'll bring you clothes, shoes for your feet,

Weapons to fight with, and I'll have you sent anywhere
You want to go – but I fear I must ask you to stay here
Because I dare not let you come to my house. The chieftains
Of this island have taken it over, and they're vicious
And violent men.

ODYSSEUS: I'm sorry, but why does no one stop them? Can't *you*
Stop them?

TELEMACHOS: I'm too young to give orders to men like that.
They wouldn't listen.

ODYSSEUS: Have you no friends? What about your brothers?

TELEMACHOS: My grandfather had one son, Odysseus. My father,
Odysseus
Had one son – myself. I am alone . . .
Eumaios, my friend, how is my mother? Has she married
Any of the suitors?

EUMAIOS: No, she won't give in. She weeps all day and all night
For Odysseus. She's wasting away, Telemachos.

TELEMACHOS: Go to her, please, and tell her I'm safely home. Say
That I'm staying here, and not to tell anyone else.

EUMAIOS: *Getting up* Trust me, sir . . . Good luck,
And god bless you.

TELEMACHOS: Goodbye, Eumaios.
            Eumaios goes out, shutting the door. The dogs howl outside
Listen to those dogs. Something has frightened them.

ODYSSEUS: Dogs can see ghosts, I've heard.

TELEMACHOS: Yes, but ghosts walk at night. This is the daytime.

ODYSSEUS: There are spirits that walk in the day as well.

TELEMACHOS: I'm going to get my sword . . .
            He goes out. Supernatural sound

ATHENE: Not a word, Odysseus. You alone can see me. No one
Else can. Pretend I'm not here . . . Now listen.
It's time for you to reveal yourself to your son.
You must plan your revenge on the suitors, then go
To the city and carry it out. I shall touch you once
And make you look like yourself again.
            Transformation effect. Supernatural sound

TELEMACHOS: *coming back* Nothing to be seen.
What's happening? The light!

ODYSSEUS: Don't be afraid.

TELEMACHOS: Stranger, who are you? The light dazzles me!
Are you a god from heaven?

ODYSSEUS: Look at me. I am no god, Telemachos. I am your father,
Back after so long. Come here, let me
Hold you, let me kiss you . . .

TELEMACHOS: You're not my father! You're some demon come
to torture me!

No man could change from old age to youth like that.
It's sorcery!

ODYSSEUS: Telemachos, don't be afraid. No other Odysseus
Will ever come. The change you see was worked
By the will of the goddess Athene. She made me
Into a tramp, and she made me young again.

TELEMACHOS: Then you really are . . .?

ODYSSEUS: Yes, Telemachos.

TELEMACHOS: Father!

ODYSSEUS: My son!

TELEMACHOS: How did you get here? Who brought you?

ODYSSEUS: A famous sailor-people. How I came here, Telemachos,
Is a story of long sea-journeys, dangers, fights
With cruel monsters, and strange happenings in magic
Islands and distant seas. You shall hear the story some day.
But now we have more important business. We must plan
The destruction of our enemies. First, how many suitors
Are there?

TELEMACHOS: Father, I know you are a great fighter, but you
cannot
Fight these suitors alone. There are nearly a hundred
Of them.

ODYSSEUS: Yes, Telemachos, we need help, and we shall have it –
From the goddess Athene. Now, here is the plan. You go
To the city tomorrow morning, and join the suitors.
I shall follow with Eumaios some time later. I shall be
Disguised again, and if any of the suitors insults
Or abuses me you are to say nothing – however much
It troubles you – nothing at all. When the time comes
I shall give you a signal, and then we shall strike.
No-one – remember this – no-one is to know I am here . . .

NARRATOR: So they continued to lay their plans until evening.
Then Eumaios returned from the city, and Athene
Once more disguised Odysseus as an old tramp. Eumaios
Was not to know yet that Odysseus was home, in case
He let the secret out. The next morning, at dawn,
Telemachos rose early, buckled on his sword, and set off
For the palace, telling Eumaios and the tramp to follow later.
It was nearly midday when they reached the city . . .

ODYSSEUS: Eumaios – can you smell that meat cooking at the
palace?

EUMAIOS: Gorging themselves again.

ODYSSEUS: Then all the more for me.

EUMAIOS: That food is for the suitors – all of it – they give
Nothing away . . . Listen . . .

Music

ODYSSEUS: Dancing.

EUMAIOS: Every day. Frivolity. Waste!

ODYSSEUS: I'm going in.

EUMAIOS: Now wait, be careful. Those suitors – they're rough
And cruel. They've no respect for age, and I wouldn't
Advise you to go anywhere near them.

ODYSSEUS: What can they do to me? Hit me? Curse me? I've
endured
Worse. I'm not afraid.

EUMAIOS: At least let me go in first to make sure no one drives you
Away.

ODYSSEUS: All right. But hurry, Eumaios, I'm hungry.
A dog whines
No, nothing for you, poor old beast, we're beggars,
Both of us.

EUMAIOS: Argos ... Argos, here, sir, here!
The dog whines
See this dog, stranger? Can you believe it, but this dog
Used to run like the wind in the hunt. Look at that back,
And those legs.

ODYSSEUS: Who does he belong to?

EUMAIOS: Odysseus ... That's odd, he likes you.

ODYSSEUS: Why odd?

EUMAIOS: Since Odysseus left he won't let anyone touch him.

ODYSSEUS: He must be twenty years old.

EUMAIOS: Yes. Odysseus reared him from a puppy, trained him,
And ever since his master went to the wars
He's been waiting – hoping to see him again.

ODYSSEUS: Argos ... Poor old Argos ... Look, Eumaios, how
filthy
He is, stained with mud, all skin and bone.

EUMAIOS: No one cares, you see, no one looks after him ... I'll
Go inside, and see if it's safe for you ...

ODYSSEUS: Argos, my faithful Argos – and so you waited ...
All these years. Well, now I'm home, Argos,
Your master is here. Now you can die in peace.
It's all right, Argos, I'm back, I'm home.

NARRATOR: Eumaios called Odysseus in from the doorstep
And gave him a sack, and told him to go round to all
The suitors and ask each of them for a scrap to eat.
Everyone laughed and ate and drank
And Odysseus went among them.

ODYSSEUS: Sir – a bite to eat, I'm a poor man ... Thank you.
Spare a crumb for a starving man ... Thank you.
I'm a poor wanderer, I haven't eaten for days ... Thank you.

NARRATOR: All the other suitors gave something, his sack was filled
   With bread and meat, until he came to Antinoös,
   And stood next to him:
ANTINOÖS: What is this lump of mange?
1st SUITOR: Never seen him before.
ANTINOÖS: What hole has he crawled out from?
ODYSSEUS: Sir, can you spare a crumb for a poor starving man?
1st SUITOR: Someone get rid of this bag of old garbage!
2nd SUITOR: Throw him out! Clear the air!
ANTINOÖS: Eumaios?
EMAIOS: Yes, Sir Antinoös?
ANTINOÖS: Did you bring this object into town?
EUMAIOS: Yes, Sir Antinoös.
ANTINOÖS: Why?
EUMAIOS: Because he's poor, he's hungry!
ANTINOÖS: Don't we have enough beggars here? Did you have to drag
   One more of these pests along? All they do
   Is gobble up our food, ruin our meal.
EUMAIOS: Sir Antinoös, you make life very hard for us servants,
   And you always seem to be picking on me. But I want you
   To know I'm not afraid of you – not so long as
   The son of the king, Telemachos, is master in this house ...
TELEMACHOS: That's enough, Eumaios, don't answer him back.
   He always starts a quarrel ... Antinoös, you set
   A fine example, don't you, shouting at a poor old
   Tramp. Give him something, I don't mind. It's my food.
   Show you can give as well as take for once.
ANTINOÖS: Keep your temper, Telemachos, and don't use that arrogant
   Voice to me! If all of us here gave that tramp what I'd
   Like to give him, he'd stay away from your house
   For a good three months.
TELEMACHOS: And what would you give him?
ANTINOÖS: This!
   He picks up a stool. The guests gasp.
TELEMACHOS: Put down that stool, Antinoös!
ODYSSEUS: Wait a moment, Prince, everyone here has been so gracious
   To me, perhaps Antinoös too will wish to show
   His true nature.
   Be generous, friend. You look so noble, you must be a king.
ANTINOÖS: Stay away from me, stand back, don't come near
   My table, scavenger!
ODYSSEUS: What a shame. Your manners don't seem to match your
   clothes ... Well – goodbye to you.

ANTINOÖS: Going so soon – without a reward
    For your insolence? I don't think so!
NARRATOR: As he spoke Antinoös picked up a stool and hurled it
    At Odysseus, and hit him on the right side, near the small
    Of his back. But Odysseus, rock steady, kept his balance,
    Never flinched under Antinoös' blow. He just shook his head,
    And walked out of the hall without a word. But his thoughts
    Were murderous.

    Meanwhile, another tramp had arrived in town. His name
    Was Iros, and he always begged in the city. An enormous man,
    Famous for his gluttony, Iros had a bloated stomach
    That nothing could fill. But for all his bulk, he was flabby.
    He arrived at the palace just as Odysseus was coming
    Out from the banqueting hall.
IROS: Out of the way, don't block the doorway, fool! Move,
    Before I have to drag you out of the way by your feet!
ODYSSEUS: Listen friend, I'm doing you no harm. This doorway
    Is wide enough for both of us – so don't be so stingy.
    I see you're a tramp, like me, but don't push me too far.
    I might get angry.
IROS: O–o–oh. What a long speech from a short piece of dirt.
    I think I'll have to give it a couple of taps with my fist
    And spill a few of those ugly teeth in the dust.
        Antinoös comes out to the doorstep
ANTINOÖS: Who's making all the noise out there . . . ?
    Laughs Look at this! . . . Come and look at this, friends . . .
        The suitors come out to the doorstep
1st SUITOR: What is it, Antinoös?
ANTINOÖS: A little after-dinner entertainment. The stranger
    And Iros are going to fight.
        Laughter
1st SUITOR: Come on, make a circle there . . .
2nd SUITOR: Off with those cloaks . . .
ANTINOÖS: I'll lay you ten to one Iros wins.
2nd SUITOR: I'm for the stranger.
1st SUITOR: No, he's just a heap of old bones. It's Iros for sure.
ANTINOÖS: Listen, friends, I have an idea. Let's put some meat
    On the fire to roast. And then whoever wins this fight
    Can eat as much as he likes. We'll elect him court beggar,
    By special appointment, with exclusive rights
    To our leftover scraps.
SUITORS: Yes, brilliant, agreed – get the meat . . .
ODYSSEUS: I'm an old man, sir, this Iros fellow is younger
    Than me. I shouldn't have to fight him.
SUITORS: Fight him, fight him! Fight or starve!

ODYSSEUS: Well, hunger makes it hard to say no. I'll fight.

ANTINOÖS: Off with your cloaks, then. You first, stranger.

ODYSSEUS: There . . . I'm ready.

Murmur from suitors

2nd SUITOR: Look at those muscles on his thighs . . .

1st SUITOR: And his shoulders – broad as a door.

2nd SUITOR: He's got arms on him like tree trunks.

1st SUITOR: Look out, Iros.

IROS: Antinoös, sir, please don't make me, I can't do it . . . please.

ANTINOÖS: Stop trembling, Iros, you're like jelly. I've wagered
Good money on you.

IROS: But look at him!

ANTINOÖS: He's an old man, you can't be afraid of *him* . . . Listen –
If you let him beat you I'll ship you off to a friend
Of mine in a foreign country who'll skin you alive
For leather bottles!

Groan from Iros

SUITORS: Stand up, Iros, into the middle . . . Come on,
Stranger – start . . . let's start . . .

NARRATOR: Odysseus and Iros faced each other and raised their
fists.
At first Odysseus wondered whether to hit Iros so hard
He would fall down dead on the spot. But after all
He decided it was better to hit him gently – then no-one
Could say he had murdered the man. So he held back,
While Iros thumped him on the right shoulder . . .

A shout

Then Odysseus cracked Iros once on the neck, just below
His ear. Iros began to spit blood, dropped howling in the dust,
Broke his teeth, and drummed the ground with his feet.
The suitors rocked with laughter, while Odysseus
Dragged Iros out of the courtyard by one foot, propped him up
Against the wall of the palace, and stuck a staff in his hand.

ODYSSEUS: Sit there, and fight off the pigs and dogs, and don't try
To be king of the beggars in future. It might be fatal
Next time.

NARRATOR: The suitors returned to their banquet, and the rest
Of the day passed in drinking and dancing, songs
And laughter, till evening came. Shadows crept through
The palace, fires of dry wood, well-seasoned timber,
Crackled, and lamps were brought and lit in the great halls.
Meanwhile the suitors, sodden with wine, began
To make fun of Odysseus.

2nd SUITOR: Listen – you see that beggar standing over
there . . . ?
He's a torch all on his own, with the light shining

Off his bald head.
>*Laughter*

1st SUITOR: Hey you – tramp! Yes, you. Come over here. How
Would you like to work – plant a few trees, hoe the ground,
That sort of thing? What if I paid you? I'd feed
And clothe you? What about it? . . . I'll bet you'd run
For your life at the first whiff of work!
>*Laughter*

ODYSSEUS: Sir, just let me get you in a meadow, a meadow of good
Long grass, give us each a sickle, and start cutting –
Then you'd see what kind of worker I am.
You think you're a big strong man now, surrounded
By your friends, this crowd of brainless nobodies.
But if Odysseus were to set foot in his palace again,
You'd all be crammed in that doorway over there, wide
As it is, running for your lives!

1st SUITOR: You insolent worm! Get out of here! Get out of
my sight!

NARRATOR: He picked up a cup, flung it at Odysseus, Odysseus
Ducked, the cup hit a servant pouring wine, the man
Gave a shout and toppled backwards on to the floor,
The cup rolled in the dust – and uproar broke loose
In the night-shadowed hall.

TELEMACHOS: *above the din* Are you mad? Stop! Stop, friends!
You've had a good meal, now go home, don't fight,
I'm not turning you out, but it's late, and . . .

2nd SUITOR: The beggar should never have come here . . .

1st SUITOR: We're fighting over a tramp now . . .

2nd SUITOR: He's spoiled the whole evening . . .

1st SUITOR: Telemachos is right. The tramp's not worth a fight.
It's time for sleep. Let's have one more drink,
Then go home.

NARRATOR: And now the last cup was poured, their thirst was
quenched
For that day, and they went home to sleep. Left alone,
Odysseus and Telemachos took all the weapons and armour
That lined the walls of the banqueting hall, and hid them
In an upstairs room. They kept back only enough
To arm themselves for their work the next day.

ODYSSEUS: There, finished. If anyone asks you what happened
To the weapons, say you put them away to save them
From rusting . . . Go to bed now, Telemachos.

TELEMACHOS: What is the strange light that follows us everywhere,
As if from a bright flame? There are no fires
Left burning . . .

ODYSSEUS: Ssh! Ask no questions, Telemachos. These are signs

That gods are near. We shall have allies in the battle
Tomorrow . . . Sleep now.

TELEMACHOS: Goodnight, father.

ODYSSEUS: Goodnight, Telemachos.

NARRATOR: Telemachos walked through the passages lit by flickering
Torches, till he came to his room. He was tired.
Sleep came quickly, and he didn't wake until dawn.
Meanwhile, back in the darkened hall, Odysseus sat
Alone, thinking, plotting death for each of the suitors.

The door opens

ODYSSEUS: Who's there?

PENELOPE: I am Penelope, Queen of Ithaca.

ODYSSEUS: Queen Penelope! I'm sorry. I didn't expect you here.

PENELOPE: You may sit down, stranger.
Servants, start clearing the tables . . .
So you are the tramp they've all been talking about.

ODYSSEUS: And you are the famous Queen Penelope, wife of Odysseus,
Whose beauty and fame I hear of wherever I go.

PENELOPE: Time has wasted my beauty, stranger, and my fame
Has meant nothing to me since my husband went to Troy.
Other men have asked me to marry them, but I think
Only of him. Every day I wait for him, every day
I weep for him . . .

ODYSSEUS: How have you answered these suitors of yours?

PENELOPE: At first I said to them: Gentlemen, wait till I have finished
Weaving this sheet for Odysseus' grave. When it is done
I shall choose one of you to be king in his place.
They waited, I wove the cloth every day, and every night
I undid the work I had done. And so it could never
Be finished. But one day they caught a servant of mine
And made her tell them what I was doing, and ever since then
I've been trapped. I have no more excuses. I have to
Be married. Now, stranger, tell me . . . who are you,
And where have you come from?

ODYSSEUS: I cannot tell you, lady, there is too much sorrow
In my story, too much pain. But I will tell you this:
Odysseus is coming home, I swear he is. He is not far
From you now.

PENELOPE: No, stranger, that will never be. You are kind,
You want to give me hope, make me happy. Or perhaps
You want a reward . . . I don't know. All I know is –
He will never come back. There are no signs, no messages.
He has gone for ever.

Servants, bring a bowl, bring water and towels,
And prepare a bed for the stranger.
ODYSSEUS: Thank you, my lady, but soft sheets, and warm water,
Are not for me. I'm a poor rough man, I'm not used
To luxury If you have some old and trusted servant,
Someone whose life has been as hard as mine, she
Can look after me.
PENELOPE: As you wish, stranger.
                calling Eurycleia!
                to Odysseus
This is a good and faithful old woman. She nursed
Odysseus, when he was a baby, and she nursed my own son.
Eurycleia, look after our guest, wash his feet,
While I attend to tomorrow's banquet . . .
NARRATOR: While Penelope's servants cleaned the great hall
And swept the floor, Eurycleia quietly washed the dirt
From Odysseus' feet.
ODYSSEUS: Why are you weeping, nurse? Does my old body
And all this dirt offend you?
EURYCLEIA: No.
ODYSSEUS: What is it, then?
EURYCLEIA: I have seen many men come here, from all parts of
    the world,
But none of them looked so much like Odysseus as you.
ODYSSEUS: You may be right. I have heard it said we are very
    alike.
EURYCLEIA: Give me your other foot . . . Now the knee . . .
ODYSSEUS: *sharply* No!
EURYCLEIA: Why not, master? This my work . . . There, soon
    Have the dirt off . . . Now . . . Ah . . .!
ODYSSEUS: What is it?
EURYCLEIA: This scar, here . . . just above the knee . . .
ODYSSEUS: I've fought many battles, I have many scars. That one,
Now let me see . . .
EURYCLEIA: Odysseus had a scar, in just the same place . . .
ODYSSEUS: I got that one fighting the . . . what was their name . . .?
EURYCLEIA: He got it hunting as a child, the same leg – yes!
Now I see. You! You are . . .
ODYSSEUS: Ssh!
                She drops the bowl.
                Odysseus claps his hand over her mouth
Do you want to kill me? No one must know
I'm here, not even Penelope. Do you understand?
Now, I don't take my hand off your mouth till you promise
You won't say a word. Promise!
                She mumbles

Nod your head.
> *She mumbles*

All right.

EURYCLEIA: *In a whisper* What makes you talk such nonsense,
child?
Do you think I'd betray you? I'm the only one here
That's loyal. Those girls, those young vipers,
I could tell you some things about *them*!

ODYSSEUS: Quiet! Penelope's coming back, she'll hear us!

PENELOPE: *approaching* Stranger, I have made up my mind.
Tomorrow
I'll choose a husband from among the suitors. Odysseus
Is never coming back.

ODYSSEUS: How will you choose?

PENELOPE: I'll give them a test, some trial of strength and skill.

ODYSSEUS: Queen Penelope, wait for Odysseus, he'll come home.

PENELOPE: You are welcome to stay and watch the test tomorrow,
Stranger . . . Goodnight now, sleep well . . . Odysseus
Will never come back . . . never . . .

NARRATOR: And Penelope went to her room, where she had wept
So many sleepless hours for the husband she loved.
But sleep comes to everyone, and it came at last
To Penelope, stilling her tears and bringing rest
To her weeping eyes.
In the darkened hall Odysseus lay, on a pile of sheepskins,
But he did not sleep. He was thinking, planning, scheming.
Tomorrow was the day. Tomorrow he would have to fight,
And he was afraid. He was alone, one man, and his enemies
Were many. He needed help, he needed luck, he needed
The goddess Athene. But she was an immortal spirit
Who obeyed no man. She would come if she wished;
If she did not, nothing could save Odysseus. At last,
Near dawn, he slept.

ODYSSEY

VI The Bending of the Bow

CAST:

Narrator
Odysseus
Penelope, his wife
Telemachos, his son
Eurycleia, his old nurse
Eumaios, the swineherd
Philoitios, a servant
Medon, a servant
Antinoös
Leodes
Eurymachos
1st Suitor

NARRATOR: The day for the trial of strength had come. The suitors
    Were drinking and eating as usual in Odysseus' palace,
    While Odysseus himself, disguised as a tramp, sat
    At one side, and watched.
    Penelope went to the armoury and brought out a huge bow
    Which Odysseus had won in war, with a quiverful of sharp
    Arrows. Then she went down to the great hall, where the suitors
    Were sitting.
        Noise of banquet, which quietens suddenly
PENELOPE: My lords, every day you come to this house. Every day
    You eat and drink and enjoy yourselves, and the only thing
    You ever say to me is, 'When will you marry?'
    Very well, suitors, today I shall decide.
        Reaction from the suitors
    Do you all see this bow? It belonged to Odysseus.
    I now challenge you all to a trial of strength. The winner
    Will be my husband. Here is what you have to do.
    First, bend this bow. Then, string it. Then, shoot an arrow
    Through twelve axe-heads which I shall set in a row
    In the ground. Whoever can do this best – he is the man
    I shall marry.
        Reaction
    Eumaios, take the bow, and give it to the suitors . . .
    What's the matter?
EUMAIOS: It makes me sad, your majesty, when you talk of
    marriage.
PENELOPE: Do it, Eumaios. I've decided.
        Eumaios carries the bow to the suitors
ANTINOÖS: Here, Eumaios, don't look like that. Let's see the bow.
1st SUITOR: Cheer up, Eumaios. All you stupid peasants are
    alike –
    You can only take in what you see in front of you.
LEODES: Look, he's crying. A woman gets married, and he goes
    Into mourning!
ANTINOÖS: Either sit and eat in silence, or else go outside
    With your tears – and leave the bow in here for the men.
EUMAIOS: Here, take it! Let's see who's man enough to bend it!
    I'm going.
SUITORS: Give it to me . . . let me see it . . .
TELEMACHOS: Wait, gentlemen. As Odysseus' son, I would like
    To try the bow first.
NARRATOR: The axe-heads were set in the earth, one behind the
    other,
    In a long trench. Then Telemachos picked up the bow
    And tried to bend it. Three times he struggled with it,
    And three times he had to give up. On the fourth try

He used all his strength and came close to succeeding,
But a shake of the head from Odysseus stopped him,
Though he longed to prove his strength. Telemachos
Put down the bow.

TELEMACHOS: Well, there it is. I'm weak and useless. Or else
I'm too young. You others can try. See if you're stronger.
The contest is open!

Reaction from suitors

ANTINOÖS: We'll do this in order, friends. One at a time
Starting from the end of the table . . . Leodes, you first . . .

Pause while Leodes strains and grunts

LEODES: No good. If anyone thinks they're going to marry the
queen
By bending this bow, they'd better start looking
For another wife. It can't be done.

ANTINOÖS: Not by you. It takes a man. Next.

Another suitor tries

1st SUITOR: I can't either. It must be the weather today.

ANTINOÖS: Or the wine you've drunk. Next.

NARRATOR: Meanwhile Odysseus slipped out of the hall and into
The courtyard, where he found Eumaios talking
To another servant, a herdsman, Philoitios.

ODYSSEUS: Eumaios – and you, sir, what is your name?

PHILOITIOS: Philoitios.

ODYSSEUS: Let me ask you something – both of you. What
Would you do if Odysseus came back?

EUMAIOS: How could he?

ODYSSEUS: He might, when you least expect him . . . You,
Philoitios,
What would you do? Fight for him? Or join the suitors?

PHILOITIOS: Fight for Odysseus, of course.

ODYSSEUS: Eumaios?

EUMAIOS: If by some miracle my master came home, you'd have
no need
To ask a question like that!

ODYSSEUS: I believe you . . . Come closer . . .
Look at this scar on my leg. I got it when I was a child,
Hunting in the forests . . .

EUMAIOS: Master! . . . My dear master . . .

PHILOITIOS: King Odysseus – how did you . . . I mean, when
did you . . . ?

ODYSSEUS: Later – we'll talk later. Quickly now, before someone
Sees us here, let me tell you my plan. I must
Get that bow in my hands somehow. That's your job,
Eumaios. You must find a way of giving it to me.
As soon as I have hold of it, tell one of the women

To shut the doors of the great hall and lock them tight.
Meanwhile you, Philoitios, slip out here and bar
The gates of the courtyard . . . Now, we must not
Be seen together, so I'll go in first, you come after me . . .

NARRATOR: Back in the hall, Odysseus went to the seat he had left.
His two servants followed a few minutes after. The suitor
Who had the bow in his hands now was called Eurymachos.
He was holding it up to the fire, hoping the heat
Would make it more easy to bend. But even so,
He could not make it give an inch.

EURYMACHOS: *gasping, out of breath* It's beaten me, I'm aching
all over!
Well, I've lost a wife – not that I care about that –
There are plenty more girls in Greece – but to think
I'm so much weaker than Odysseus – that's the shameful
Part of it. And everyone knows it now.

ANTINOÖS: That's not so, Eurymachos, you don't believe it yourself.
Today is a holiday, sacred to the gods – who could bend
A bow on a day like this? Leave it there. Let's wait
Till tomorrow. We'll try again, and one of us is sure
To succeed.

SUITORS: Good idea . . . more wine . . . servants, bring the cups . . .
Fill them up . . . give everyone more wine . . .

ODYSSEUS: Excuse me, gentlemen, suitors of the most noble queen,
By all means leave the trial of the bow until tomorrow,
And let god decide who shall be victor. But I should like
To measure my strength against yours. Are my old limbs
As strong as they used to be? Give me the bow
And let me see.

A chorus of derisive shouts and jeers

ANTINOÖS: Your wits have gone the same way as your youth,
stranger.
Out of all the tramps that pester us here, you alone
Have been allowed to eat with us, and listen
To our brilliant conversation. What more do you want?
Do you want to join in? The wine has washed your brains
Away. Drink up and shut up.

PENELOPE: You ought to be ashamed of yourself, Antinoös. You
Are as much of a guest in this house as he is.
What if the stranger does bend the bow? What's that to you?
He's strong, he comes of a good family. Give him the bow.
Let's see what he can do.

TELEMACHOS: Mother, I am the man in this house, and I decide
Who may handle this bow and who may not. You are a woman.
Go to your rooms, please, and work at your woman's
Business. Leave bows and weapons of war to me.

Pause – murmur

NARRATOR: Penelope had nothing to say. Her son's authority
Amazed her, and she left the hall in silence. Back
In her room she closed the door, and wept – wept
For Odysseus, her dear husband, till merciful sleep
Closed her eyes.
That sleep was sent by the goddess Athene, who wanted
Penelope to know nothing about what was to happen.

But now, in the banqueting hall, Eumaios had seen
His chance, and picked up the bow.

1st SUITOR: Eumaios – where are you going with that?

LEODES: Be careful! Put it down!

TELEMACHOS: Eumaios, you cannot obey everyone. Obey me. I
Am master in this house. Give the bow to the tramp.
Outburst of comment from suitors

EUMAIOS: Here you are, sir . . .

ODYSSEUS: *In a whisper* Careful!

EUMAIOS: Sir beggar, I mean . . .

ODYSSEUS: *In a whisper* Now. Tell the women now!

EUMAIOS: *In a whisper* Eurycleia, you are to close all the doors
To the hall – and whatever you hear inside, shouts, blows,
Don't pay any attention. Just go on with your work.

NARRATOR: The old nurse obeyed without a word, and quietly
locked
The doors of the hall. Meanwhile Philoitios, the herdsman,
Slipped out and tied the doors of the courtyard shut
With a tough piece of ship's rigging. Now the suitors
Were trapped.
In the hall, Odysseus was turning the bow over and over
In his hands.

1st SUITOR: Look at the tramp. Quite a connoisseur of bows.
Perhaps he collects them.

EURYMACHOS: Must have a few of his own at home.

LEODES: Perhaps he wants one like it, and he's studying
The way it's made.

NARRATOR: While the suitors joked, Odysseus, who knew more
tricks
Than they ever would, examined and felt the great bow.
An expert musician, who both plays and sings to his lyre,
Takes no time to stretch a string round a new peg
And tighten the sheep-gut at both ends –
And it was as simple as that for Odysseus to bend
And string the great bow – it was done!
He picked it up, and with his right hand he tested
The string. It sang out sweet as the trill of a swallow.

The suitors felt a pang of fear run through them.
They all blenched ... There was a roll of thunder,
And Odysseus, who had seen so much suffering and endured it
All, felt a leap of gladness, because he knew the sign
Was meant for him, from the mysterious will of Zeus.
He picked up a swift arrow, which lay ready nearby,
Laid the arrow against the bow, gripped it by its notch,
Drew back the bowstring, aimed, and, without getting up
From the chair where he sat, shot it straight
At the axe-heads. It went right through, without touching
A single one, and flew out at the other end.
Odysseus nodded. Telemachos buckled on his sword,
Seized a spear, and ran over to stand beside his father.
Odysseus tossed aside his ragged cloak and leapt up
On to the raised stair at the entrance to the hall.
He spilled the quiverful of arrows on the floor at his feet.

ODYSSEUS: Suitors – here is a new trial of strength for you,
And this one will be to the death! I shall aim
At another target, one that no man has ever hit before.

NARRATOR: He sent an arrow whizzing straight at Antinoös.
At that second Antinoös was raising a golden cup
To his lips, ready to drink. The one thing he never expected
(How could he?) Was that someone would strike him dead
In the middle of that crowded banquet. The arrow
Plunged deep into his throat, and came out at the other side.
He toppled over to one side, the cup fell
From his stiffening hand, and a thick rivulet of blood
Gushed from his nostrils. As he fell his heel pushed over
The table. Bread, meat, pieces of cooked pastry
Were scattered all over the floor, and the suitors
Let out a roar. They all thought, the fools,
That Odysseus had killed Antinoös by accident.
They didn't know he meant to murder every one of them there.

1st SUITOR: Stranger, that's the last time you'll touch a bow.

LEODES: You've shot your way into certain death.

EURYMACHOS: The man you killed was one of our greatest nobles.
You'll be feeding the vultures for that.

ODYSSEUS: Dogs! Did you think I'd never come home from Troy?
Pause, murmurs of 'Odysseus ... Odysseus'
Yes – Odysseus! Now let the feast begin in earnest!
Today the banquet is in *my* honour!

EURYMACHOS: If you really are Odysseus, King of Ithaca, you have
A right to be angry. Bad things have been done
In this house, no one denies it. But look, there lies
The man who started it all – Antinoös. What he wanted
Was not your wife – but to be king in your place. Well,

Now he's dead, so spare the rest of your subjects.
As for all we've eaten and drunk, we'll pay for it
Out of our own treasuries.

ODYSSEUS: Yes, Eurymachos, you'll pay – but not with money.
You'll pay with your lives. All of you! Now choose –
Run or fight!

EURYMACHOS: Friends – draw your swords, tip over the tables,
And take cover from his arrows. Let's all attack
At once, and beat him from the door. We can do it
If we do it together. Follow me!

NARRATOR: Eurymachos drew his sharp sword, and lunged at
    Odysseus
With a fierce battle cry. Odysseus met him with an arrow
Right in his chest, and the point went through to his liver.
He dropped the sword and fell sideways over a table,
Pitching food and cups to the floor. His head bumped
On the ground, and his feet kicked in agony. A mist
Clouded his eyes. He was dead.
Next came a great strong man, Amphinomos, who sprang
On Odysseus brandishing his sword, and was about to drive him
From the doorway when Telemachos brought him down
From behind with a spear between his shoulders. The tip
Poked out from his chest, and he fell face downwards
With a crash. Telemachos rushed back to join his father,
Leaving his spear in the corpse, in case one of the suitors
Took him off guard.

TELEMACHOS: Father, we need more armour. We have to give
    spears
And shields to Eumaios and Philoitios.

ODYSSEUS: Yes, get them. But hurry. I can't hold off the suitors
For long by myself.

NARRATOR: Telemachos ran to the chamber where the weapons
    were stored,
And brought back helmets and shields and spears
For the two peasants. They quickly put on the armour,
And stood next to Odysseus. Now they were four.
So long as the arrows lasted Odysseus could pick off
The suitors one by one, and they fell like mowed grass.
But soon the arrows were all used up, and Odysseus
Had to lay down his bow and take up two bronze-tipped
Spears. Meanwhile a goat-herd, Melanthios, who was fighting
On the side of the suitors, had discovered a way
Over the rafters of the hall into the room where Odysseus
And his son had hidden the armour. He climbed up there
And returned with twelve shields, twelve helmets,
And twelve spears. They were soon in the hands

Of the suitors, and he set out for more. When he saw
His enemies aiming those long spears at him, Odysseus
Felt a tremor of fear shake his limbs.

ODYSSEUS: Telemachos, one of the women has betrayed us.

TELEMACHOS: No, father, it was my fault. I left the door
Of the storeroom open. We should have put someone
There to guard it.
Eumaios, go and find out who's giving the suitors armour.

EUMAIOS: I think it's Melanthios. I saw him creep away just now.
What shall we do with him? Kill him?

ODYSSEUS: No. Just take him prisoner. You and Philoitios go.
I'll hold off the suitors here with Telemachos.

NARRATOR: Eumaios and the herdsman went up to the storeroom,
And there they found Melanthios searching for weapons
In the back of the room. He didn't hear them coming.
They waited for him, one on each side of the doorway,
And grabbed him as he tiptoed out, his arms loaded
With shields and spears. They threw him to the ground,
Trussed him up, and left him there, locked in the room.
They went back to help Odysseus, and once more they were four.
The surviving suitors knew now they were fighting
For their lives. They were trained warriors, brave
And tough. Their next attack was a volley of six spears.
One of them crashed into the doorpost of the great hall,
Another stuck in the door itself, a third glanced
Harmlessly off the wall, and the other three went wide.
Then Odysseus and his men replied with four spears
Of their own. Four of the suitors were hit, and the rest
Went scurrying back to the far end of the hall.
Once more they rallied, aimed, and attacked. This time
One of the spears struck Telemachos on his wrist,
And the bronze point opened a deep gash; another
Grazed Eumaios on his shoulder above his shield,
Then flew up in the air and clattered to the ground.
Odysseus plunged into the struggle to beat them back,
And the suitors retreated as spear after wounding spear
Hurtled towards them. Now Athene brought her help.
She blew a spirit of unreasoning dread through the palace,
And drove the suitors into a wild panic. They lost
Their will to fight. They were like a herd of cattle,
Blundering about the hall. Odysseus and his men leapt
Down on them like vultures, chasing them
All through the building, hacking right and left,
And the air was filled with the ghastly sound
Of cracking skulls, and the floor was all streaming
With blood. At last there was silence.

Odysseus surveyed his house. Not a single one of the suitors
Had escaped alive. They were all dead, heaped
In the dust and blood, like a shoal of fishes tipped
Out of a net onto the sand.

TELEMACHOS: Father – where's Medon?

ODYSSEUS: Who?

TELEMACHOS: Medon. He used to carry our messages.

ODYSSEUS: I don't know. No-one here looks alive.

TELEMACHOS: Medon didn't do any harm. He was always respectful,

And he looked after me when I was small . . . Eumaios?

EUMAIOS: Yes, sir?

TELEMACHOS: Did you kill Medon, the messenger?

EUMAIOS: No, sir.

TELEMACHOS: Look for him, see if he's dead.

MEDON: *muffled* Here I am.

TELEMACHOS: Where?

MEDON: Here.

ODYSSEUS: It's coming from under that table.

TELEMACHOS: Come out, Medon, out from under those rugs . . .

MEDON: *emerging* Sir, young master, please don't kill me,

I know you're angry with the suitors, but I've done no harm.

ODYSSEUS: *laughing* Don't be afraid. My son has saved your life.

Go outside, and leave us alone . . .

MEDON: Thank you, sir, thank you, young master, god bless you.

NARRATOR: Odysseus called in the servant girls and set them to work

Cleaning the chairs and tables, sponging the blood
Off the walls and furniture, and spreading sawdust
On the floor. Meanwhile the four men hauled the bodies
Out into the courtyard and piled them up in rows.
Then Odysseus washed himself clean,
Went back into the house, and called his old nurse,
Eurycleia.

ODYSSEUS: Go and wake Penelope. Tell her to come down here.

EURYCLEIA: Yes, master, at once. It's time she knew you were home.

ODYSSEUS: You, girls, finish cleaning up in here. Light a fire
For the queen.

Eurycleia climbs the stairs, stops, knocks on the door

EURYCLEIA: Mistress . . .

Knock

Penelope, child, are you awake?

PENELOPE: *behind door, yawns* Who is it?

EURYCLEIA: Penelope, come and see something.

PENELOPE: What is there to see?

EURYCLEIA: Something you've prayed for these twenty years past.
　Odysseus has come home.
　　　　　Gasp, door opens
PENELOPE: *close, angry* Eurycleia, God has made you raving mad!
　How could you torture me with a story like this
　When you know how my heart is breaking? And I was sleeping
　So beautifully . . .
EURYCLEIA: This story is true, Penelope.
PENELOPE: Go away and stop playing tricks on me.
EURYCLEIA: The stranger – the stranger was him all the time.
PENELOPE: Eurycleia, I warn you, just because you're an old
　　woman . . .
EURYCLEIA: And the suitors are all dead!
PENELOPE: Dead . . . No, – it can't be! It's not true.
EURYCLEIA: I heard their screams, I saw their bodies.
PENELOPE: Then a god must have killed them. Odysseus is dead,
　He died long ago, far away from here.
EURYCLEIA: Child, the husband you say will never come back
　Is downstairs, this very minute, at his own fireside.
　I've seen the scar on his leg. If I'm wrong, show me
　No mercy, and put me to death!
PENELOPE: Dear nurse, you're old and wise, but can even you
　See through the disguise of a demon or a spirit?
　Well, I'll come downstairs. If the suitors are really
　Dead I must see the man who killed them.
NARRATOR: As Penelope left her room and walked down the stairs
　Her heart was leaping wildly. Should she doubt this man?
　How should she greet him?
　With questions . . .?
　Or with kisses . . .?
　She came to the hall – crossed the threshold – went over
　To the fireplace – and sat down in the firelight
　Opposite Odysseus.
　On the far side of the room Odysseus leaned back
　In his chair against a tall pillar, staring at the ground
　Between his feet, waiting to see whether his wife
　Would speak to him now that she had seen him herself.
　For some time they sat like that, in silence.
　Sometimes Penelope would glance at his face and think
　She recognised him. Then she would look at the wretched rags
　He wore, and refuse to believe it. At last
　Telemachos burst out . . .
TELEMACHOS: Mother! Mother of stone! Why don't you go up
　　to him?
　Look, it's my father! Twenty whole years
　He's been away, and you sit there like a marble statue!

PENELOPE: My son, if this is really Odysseus, we shall know
  Each other. We have signs, secret signs we have told
  To nobody else.
ODYSSEUS: Leave us alone, Telemachos, your mother will find out
  Who I am in her own way . . . And in case the news
  Of the battle in here gets out too soon, have musicians
  Start playing. Then anyone going past the palace
  Will say: 'Listen to the suitors – still enjoying
  Themselves, still at their games and dancing!'
TELEMACHOS: Come, Eumaios, Philoitios, we'll make everyone
    think
  We're having a wedding at last . . .
      They go. Music begins to play

ODYSSEUS: Well, dear queen, you must have been born with a
    heart
  Of flint. No other woman could keep so aloof
  From her husband when he came back home after twenty years
  Of fighting and travels. Well, I'm going to sleep . . .
  Eurycleia, make up my bed . . . This wife of mine
  Is cold steel to her marrow . . .
PENELOPE: Yes, Eurycleia, make up his bed – the bed Odysseus
  Himself built – which we had moved out of the room –
  And spread rugs and blankets and warm fluffy sheepskins . . .
ODYSSEUS: What? What did you say? MOVED it! Now I'm
    angry!
  No-one could move that bed, the way I made it.
  There was a young olive tree, thick and firm
  As a pillar. I built the bedroom of my palace
  Around that tree, and I made its trunk one of the four
  Posts of my bed. My bed, woman, my marriage bed
  Was rooted in the earth, firm, fixed, immovable!
  Who has chopped it down?
PENELOPE: Odysseus – dear Odysseus – don't glare at me.
  No-one has moved your bed. I only said that to test you,
  Because you and you alone could know the secret
  Of the olive tree. Don't be angry with me for not speaking
  To you when I first saw you. I was frozen with fear –
  Fear that someone had come to deceive me with stories
  Again. But now I believe it's you, I believe
  With all my heart and soul! . . . Odysseus . . .!
ODYSSEUS: Come here, Penelope, come here, my love, my dear
    wife . . .
NARRATOR: They ran into each other's arms, and held each other,
  And wept, while the gay music played on in the palace.

Then Odysseus told Penelope the whole story
Of his wanderings. It took him all that day,
And most of the night, to finish the story, and at last
They went to the room Odysseus had built round
The olive tree, the room where his bed was planted,
And there, at last, husband and wife again, after
Twenty years apart, they slept.
Odysseus was home for good.

Pronunciation

Achilles A-*kill*-ees
Aeneas Ee-*nee*-as
Aiaie Eye-*eye*-ee
Aiolos *Eye*-oll-os
Ajax *Ay*-jax
Alcinoös Al-sin-*owe*-os
Amphinomos Am-fi-*nom*-os
Andromache An-*drom*-acky
Antinoös An-tin-*owe*-os
Archeptolemos Ar-kept-*olly*-mos
Asios As-*ee*-os
Astyanax As-*tie*-an-ax
Athene Ath-*ee*-nee

Briseis Bry-*say*-is

Charybdis Ka-*rib*-dis
Chryseis Kry-*say*-is
Circe *Sir*-see
Cyclops *Sy*-klops

Diomedes *Die*-owe-meed-ees
Dolon *Doll*-own

Epeios Ep-*ay*-os
Eumaios Yoo-*my*-os
Eurycleia Yoo-rik-*lay*-a
Eurylochos Yoo-*rill*-ok-os
Eurymachos Yoo-*rim*-ak-os

Hades *Hay*-deez
Hecuba *Hek*-yoo-ba
Hephaistos Hef-*eye*-stos
Hermes *Her*-mees

Iris *Eye*-riss
Iros *Eye*-ros
Ithaca *Ith*-ak-a

Kalchas *Kal*-kas
Koön *Ko*-own

Laodamas Lay-*odd*-a-mas
Lotos *Low*-tos
Leodes Le-*ode*-ees

Macedonia *Mass*-i-*doe*-nee-a
Medon *Mee*-don
Melanthios Mel-*anth*-ee-os
Menelaus Men-ell-*ay*-us
Moly *Mole*-i

Nausicaa *Naw*-sik-*ay*-a
Nestor *Nest*-or

Odysseus Odd-*iss*-yoos
Olympos Oll-*imp*-os

Paris *Pa*-ris
Patroklos Pat-*rok*-los
Peleus *Peel*-yoos
Phaeacia Fi-*ay*-shee-a
Philistios Fi-*list*-ee-os
Poseidon *Poss*-*eye*-don
Priam *Pry*-am

Rhesos *Ree*-sos

Scamander Skam-*and*-er
Scylla *Sill*-a
Skaian *Sky*-an
Sinon *Sin*-own

Telemachos Tell-*em*-ak-os
Teukros Tyoo-kros
Thetis *Thet*-is

Zeus Zyoos